FAUST

Borgo Press Books by ADOLPHE D'ENNERY

The Children of Captain Grant: A Play in Five Acts (with Jules Verne)
Faust: A Play in XIV Scenes
Michael Strogoff: A Play in Five Acts (with Jules Verne)
The Voyage Through the Impossible: A Play in Three Acts (with Jules Verne)

FAUST

A PLAY IN XIV SCENES

ADOLPHE D'ENNERY

Translated and Adapted by Frank J. Morlock

THE BORGO PRESS
MMXII

FAUST

Copyright © 2012 by Frank J. Morlock

FIRST EDITION

Published by Wildside Press LLC

www.wildsidebooks.com

DEDICATION

This play is dedicated to Gerry Tetrault,
For fifty-odd years of friendship.

CONTENTS

CAST OF CHARACTERS 9

SCENE I: Prologue 11

SCENE II 41

SCENE III 61

SCENE IV 73

SCENE V 79

SCENE VI 97

SCENE VII 105

SCENE VIII 137

SCENE IX 147

SCENE X 149

SCENE XI 171

SCENE XII 191

SCENE XIII 195

SCENE XIV 203

ABOUT THE AUTHOR 205

CAST OF CHARACTERS

Faust

Mephistopheles

Valentin

Wagner

Fridolin

An Indian

An Angel

Second Indian

A student

Third Indian

First worker

Second worker

Marguerite

Sulphurine

The Sorceress

Olympia

Daphne

A young woman

Sybille

Gudulle

Lisette

The statue of Helen

(Workers, strollers, sorcerers, monkeys, cats, demons, Indians, people, slaves, pages, lords and ladies, guests, coryphées, Nubians, guards, Palanquin bearers)

Characters in the Apotheosis

SCENE I
PROLOGUE

Faust's Laboratory.

To the left an entrance facing the public, one descends from it into the stage by a few steps—on the same side at the back, a credenza on which are books, papers. To the right an alchemists' furnace—on the same side a window and a door.

Wagner

(Entering—holding an open book) Fridolin! Fridolin!

Fridolin

Master Wagner?

Wagner

For a moment leave the furnace and come closer.

Fridolin

(Who is at the furnace, a bellows in hand) Here I am, Master Wagner—

Wagner

My lad, who do you think is the wisest—me or Master Faust?

Fridolin

I think it's you, Master.

Wagner

And why do you think that it's me, my friend?

Fridolin

Because you told me so, Master.

Wagner

Imbecile! (Charging tone) Go blow! To the furnace! To the furnace!

Fridolin

I'm going—I'm going.

Wagner

Stop. (Pulling him by the ear) What, double moron that you are, you don't understand that Master Faust has spent his life in studying the causes and effects to fathom what is, while as for me, I intend to create that which is not.

Fridolin

I understand it very well, Master, since you tell me so.

Wagner

Well! He studies what is.

Fridolin

Yes.

Wagner

I study what is not.

Fridolin

Yes—

Wagner

Therefore, I am more wise than he.

Fridolin

Yes—

Wagner

Much more wise than he, because....

Fridolin

Because you tell no so—

Wagner

Brute! Go to your furnaces—!

Fridolin

Yes, Master. (Noise of rapping outside) Master, they're knocking.

Wagner

Well—! Go open.

Fridolin

(Going calmly to the furnace) Ah. (Shouting) Come in!

Magnus

(Entering) Is this the dwelling of the savant—Doctor Faustus?

Fridolin

This is it.

Magnus

I wish to speak to him.

Wagner

The Doctor is absent—if you'd like to come back?

Magnus

No, I'm going to wait for him. (Sits in a large armchair)

Wagner

Say, there, that's the Master's armchair.

Magnus

It must be that of his guest, of his oldest friend.

Wagner

His friend?

Magnus

I am Doctor Magnus. (Wagner and Fridolin bow with respect) It's been thirty years since Doctor Faustus and I have been writing each other without ever seeing each other. We are indeed both old, and I didn't want to die without having shaken the hand of the greatest Savant of Germany—

It's for that I've come express from Nurnberg.

Fridolin

(To Wagner) The greatest—? Then it's not you?

Wagner

(After having made a gesture to Fridolin to remain at his furnace) Is it really true that the science of Master Faustus is so great?

Magnus

Why that question?

Wagner

Because I think I'm as learned as he—

Fridolin

More!

Magnus

(To Wagner) You! And from where comes it that you scorn your Master so much?

Wagner

Why I don't scorn him, I esteem myself.

Fridolin

More.

Magnus

Speak, then.

Wagner

I don't place Master Faust above me because I think with a little study I will end by doing what he has done, while he will never do—what I will do.

Fridolin

There you go!

Magnus

What's that?

Wagner

You know that God created man in his image?

Magnus

I know that in their pride men pretend that.

Wagner

Well, I intend to create a living being. Understand, Doctor, I intend to create someone in my image; finally I intend to give it life.

Fridolin

Heavens! You are going to get married?

Wagner

Fie! That's an old way which besides they could contest the invention with me.

Fridolin

Ah! It's not possible.

Wagner

It's a hackneyed way.

Magnus

Hackneyed! Hackneyed! But which could really be used for a long time.

Wagner

As for me, I intend to give existence to it, without associating a simple woman in my glory.

Fridolin

Ah! Bah!

Wagner

Yes—with the aid of combined substances, extracts and essences—

Fridolin

That's fine that is—And what sex will he or she be?

Wagner

I intend to create something lovable, gracious, spiritual—

Fridolin

It's a woman—

Wagner

A model of submission.

Fridolin

It's a man—

Wagner

Faithful.

Fridolin

It's a dog in that case.

Wagner

I've exhausted all the formulas; I've been ready to succeed, but at the supreme moment, I always lack something—

Magnus

You lack spirit.

Fridolin

There you go.

Wagner

What do you mean, spirit?

Magnus

(Rising) The breath, the soul, in the end life—

Wagner

Yes, life—! Absolutely, it only lacked that to animate my creature.

Magnus

It's a little thing. (Giving him a flask) And by pouring this into the mix—the contents of this little viol—I believe it will be able to guarantee you success.

Wagner

What—in there?

Magnus

It's what you lack.

Wagner

There's spirit in there?

Magnus

Yes.

Wagner

There's soul, breath—?

Magnus

(Cocking his ear) Be quiet. Hide that very carefully—your Master—

Wagner

My Master! Ah! I am going to be his, now. (Goes to right)

Faust

(Enters, bouquet in hand) I was able to master the storm; I was able to turn away lightning—and I am unable to restore to these flowers a little of their lost freshness—(Places the bouquet to the left) (Noticing Magnus) A stranger!

Magnus

A friend! Magnus, your old correspondent from Nurnberg.

Faust

Magnus. (To Fridolin and Wagner) Leave us.

Wagner

(Aside) Patience! I will soon have my slave whom I'll order about in my turn.

Faust

Will you be gone? Obey!

Fridolin

Yes, Master.

Wagner

(To Fridolin) Get going, obey! (He leaves)

Fridolin

(Aside, following him) What could I indeed create? Me, too! (Faust brings up an armchair for Magnus)

Faust

(Sitting to the right, Magnus to the left) The savant, the illustrious Magnus at my home.

Magnus

Illustrious, savant—! My friend, we give ourselves these titles before the vulgar; but when we are alone, let's agree that the greatest among us is, indeed, little, and that the wisest know they don't know very much.

Faust

Yes, yes—to know that one doesn't know, that's the most real fruit of human study.

Wagner

No one is here to hear us. You've consecrated your whole life to work—are you quite satisfied with the result of your long career?

Faust

(Shaking his hand) And you?

Magnus

Alas! So many fine years wasted, friend! I wanted to appreciate the mysteries of creation.

Faust

We pale when confronted with the unknown secrets of nature.

Magnus

And backs bent and head whitened—leaning over our books—

Faust

And one day, you raise your eyes, everything has changed around you, time has fled, carrying off the objects of your affection, all that made you smile, all that you used to love, and if, by chance, a friend survives who extends to you his old, trembling hand—(He extends his hand and presses Magnus's) There are so many regrets in this silent embrace.

Magnus

And when one sees young couples who are going about joyfully, arms entwined, as they say—what have I done with my youth?

Faust

And when one hears under the big green trees, or behind the flowering briars, words of love which are exchanged, the give and take of kisses as they say to themselves: What have I done with my heart?

Magnus

Yes, study bears a bitter fruit—and that fruit is called deception.

Faust

(Rising and passing to the left) It's my fault, heaven warned me of it a hundred times. I shut my ears.

Magnus

(Ironic) Ah! Ah! Heaven spoke to you? (Rising) Health to the elect of the Lord!

Faust

God speaks to all men, for each of them he has a language. He's the God of Armies, and he speaks to soldiers in the voice of trumpets; the poet hears a celestial voice which sings in his heart; God speaks also for others in the murmur of the water, in the perfume of flowers, in the song of birds. As for me, shut in this somber laboratory, absorbed completely in study, from my youth it was the clocks that seemed to me to be speaking to me. (Gesture by Magnus) Don't smile, Doctor, I really heard what seemed celestial voices mixed with their voices of bronze; yes the clocks said to me, when I was twenty, each Sunday and at Christmas and Palm Sunday "Greetings, greetings to youth—this is the hour when everything smiles—the hour of prayer, the hour of love; it's the time when hearts choose each other, it's the time when marriages are blessed. Come pray, come love, too" And I remained plunged in study! Then arrived mature age and the voice of clocks became more grave "Greeting, greetings once more, greetings; this is the season in which the tree bears its fruit, the age man is married and a parent. Time's flying, friend don't consume your life in sterile studies, come prepare for the joys of your last years; think of choosing the arm that will support shaking feet, think of creating hearts that will pray around you, which will piously guard your memory" And I still kept working. Then old age came—why is it I no longer hear them? My house is still in the same place, the church is still nearby—and yet I no longer hear the clocks. Ah, it's been too long that I closed my heart and my ear to the advice of their friendly voices; they used to speak to me of happiness, of love, of hope—but I'm eighty years old, and no question, the clocks have nothing more to tell me.

Magnus

Yes—yes—pleasure, wealth, glory—so many treasures unknown and disdained by us.

Faust

We took a false path—our life is a failure.

Magnus

(Forcefully) And to start over.

Faust

Start over!

Magnus

We need to become young again.

Faust

To make youth bloom again.

Magnus

Why not? Nothing dies in nature. The day which ends at twilight begins again at dawn, and the tree that sees its last fruit fall, feels itself burgeoning already with new flowers. You see this bouquet withered after a month. (Passing to the left, and taking the bouquet) Well, it's going to be reborn. (Gesture by Faustus) Ah! I'm making you smile! And if I told you that a time will come when thought will cross the Ocean more rapidly than lightning, you will laugh—and you will be wrong—if I am speaking to you of a power capable to causing sleep by a single gesture, of animating simply with a glance—you will laugh—and you will be wrong—If I tell you, finally, that this living fluid which animates me is perhaps transmitted by breath, by contact, by will—you will laugh again—and you will be wrong. (He points to the bouquet which has regained all its freshness)

Faust

(Astonished as he takes it) It's true! It's true! Yes, yes—it's a great miracle, Master—but there's nothing in it that surprises me.

Magnus

Truly? Lord Faust knows the wisest doctors?

Faust

Yes, I know of one. (Going to the left) I have there a bunch of miracles made by him—a thousand times more sublime than yours—

Magnus

And this bunch?

Faust

(Presenting the Evangelist to him) Here it is—take and open it—you will find in it how the blind see, and the deaf hear—how paralytics walk, how the dead emerge from the tomb and are reborn to life—take it.

Magnus

So be it! (Goes to take the book, lets out a scream, and pushes it away) Why, what is this book?

Faust

This book? It's the Evangelist? And you!—You are Satan! (He extends the book to him; Magnus changes clothes and appearance and appears under features and costume of Mephistopheles) Out of here! Get thee away, damned one, get thee away!

Mephistopheles

Well played, my Master, you detected me.

Faust

And I order you to leave.

Mephistopheles

If you send me away fast, I might think you were afraid.

Faust

Afraid of you! Stay put.

Mephistopheles

Thanks—

Faust

Your name?

Mephistopheles

Mephistopheles.

Faust

Mephistopheles? Oh! Oh! You occupy a distinguished rank in the infernal legions.

Mephistopheles

Can we talk? (Sits down)

Faust

I know in advance what you have to say to me: you are going to propose to me the fulfillment of some wish, and you will demand my soul in exchange.

Mephistopheles

Fie! That's old and hackneyed—what you are saying to me, Doctor? Why, look at me, will you? Am I a vulgar demon? Where are my horns? Where are my claws? Am I the devil of the Sabbath? The mysterious toothless old devil of your monks? I am young. I deal in business like a gallant gentleman, not like an old usurer.

Faust

Well—explain yourself.

Mephistopheles

First of all, I disdain all contracts between us: I give and demand nothing. No, I am not proposing to you an eternal pact of damnation, an old worm-eaten parchment signed with a drop of your blood. I am coming to offer you the objects of your nightly dreams, of your secret sighs, of your endless regrets. I will give you your youth and I will demand nothing of you;

glory, love, riches, and I will ask for nothing.

Faust

But that will be for you a bargain of a dupe, and I find you indeed quite young. (He leans on the back of an armchair)

Mephistopheles

A dupe's bargain? Yes, if God made of man as your pride persuades you, a being of reason. Yes, if the insatiability of your heart does not fetch up, in love, jealousy, hate, and some little crime which will deliver your soul to me. (Rising) Yes, if in youth you have not only enthusiasm and faith, generosity in glory and charity in riches. Take from all the wealth I am offering you only the flower of purity, grand, good, and divine in them, and I will truly have made a fool's bargain. But if, as I think, man is a wretched creature who has eyes not to see, ears not to hear; if the sap of youth which is going to boil in your exhausted veins, with it the scum of evil passions, you will damn yourself indeed by yourself, and I have no need except, in advance, you assure me your soul by a good receipt or by a result to order—

Faust

I understand—and all these precious gifts you are offering me—

Mephistopheles

Well?

Faust

I refuse them.

Mephistopheles

You refuse them? What! Despite experience which will know where stop you in which the snares of hell are born? Despite your memory that I will leave living in you—this wisdom slowly acquired which will warn you of the danger.

Faust

I refuse.

Mephistopheles

You refuse to be young?

Faust

Yes.

Mephistopheles

You refuse to be handsome?

Faust

Yes.

Mephistopheles

You refuse to be loved?

Faust

Loved!—Wait—

Mephistopheles

Loved by all those to whom you say—I love you—

Faust

Shut up.

Mephistopheles

Accompanied by all the riches.

Faust

Enough.

Mephistopheles

Intoxicated by all the glory—adored by all the women—

Faust

(Forcefully) Leave me! Well—no!—talk—talk some more.

Mephistopheles

(Aside) Here we go. (Aloud) Accept, Faust, accept; say a word and you will see at your feet the souls of the most haughty and the hearts of the most tender—(Clocks sound; Faust cocks an ear) Accept, and you will choose your love affairs among the most beautiful girls.

Faust

(Moves away—Mephistopheles passes to the left) Silence, accursed one, silence! It's the voice of clocks. They are speaking to me as they used to. Listen—listen—what they are saying to me—is—"Greetings, greetings also to old age, to the man who in his long career has conquered evil passions, and to the man stronger than the demon who puts his confidence in the Lord; to the old geezer bent over the tomb who repulses with disdain the treasures of the earth, who goes to sleep in his faith, to awake glorious and resplendent in eternity." Lord!—Lord! My soul is completely yours! And you accursed one—Be gone! Be gone!

Mephistopheles

I obey; but remember that I am offering you love, riches and power—wherever you may be, I will be—call me, you will see me appear.

Faust

Holy clocks, my heart listened to you and I am going to pray in the house of the Lord. (Heads toward the door)

Mephistopheles

(Disappearing) Too late—you will call me back. (He vanishes) (Faust leaves, after a moment Fridolin and Wagner enter)

Fridolin

What's wrong? They left, Master.

Wagner

Ah! I can finally attempt the great experiment! Quick, the furnace, the bellows.

Fridolin

(Going to the furnace) There, Master, there—

Wagner

Ah! This is the supreme moment! Blow!

Fridolin

Yes, Master.

Wagner

When I think that I am going to have a woman kneaded by my hand!— My heart beats at the thought of my immense enterprise!

Fridolin

And to say that it is I who shall have blown the fire of this sublime decoction.

Wagner

To say that I shall have a slave always at my feet! Whose life will be spent forseeing all my wishes, fulfilling humbly my orders.

Fridolin

That does it, Master—that does it—Oh! I have emotions.

Wagner

You have indeed put in there all the objects on the list I gave you?

Fridolin

Yes, Master—but I didn't suspect that they were the ingredients necessary for the manufacture of a woman.

Wagner

Then—everything's on there?

Fridolin

(Showing a paper) I have the list.

Wagner

Give it to me! Let's check it. (Reading tenderly) The heart of a turtle—dove—

Fridolin

Quite small, quite small! Not much heart, that, Master.

Wagner

My friend, don't ask the impossible. (Reading) The sweetness of a lamb.

Fridolin

I put in the whole lamb.

Wagner

You did well—I insist that she be very sweet—(Reading) Beauty.

Fridolin

I think you will be content.

Wagner

(Continuing) Grace, trickiness, cunning, cleverness.

Fridolin

Oh! A bitch!

Wagner

All this in moderation—not too much bitch.

Fridolin

It has to be part of the account.

Wagner

Finally, soul, the breath—Ah! This is what's missing.

Fridolin

The viol of Doctor Magnus.

Wagner

(Showing it) There it is. (Fridolin wants to grasp it and looks at it with religion) He assures that this must animate my creature. Let's busy ourselves quickly with the great work—of my creation. Blow! (He pours in the contents of the viol—an explosion is heard. The cauldron bursts. Wagner falls to the left and Fridolin to the right, screaming, face to the ground. Sulphurine appears) (Sulphurine emerges from the cauldron, looks around her with astonishment and runs from one object to the next)

Wagner

(Raising his head) Fridolin! Fridolin!

Fridolin

(Raising his head) Master?

Wagner

Did I succeed?

Fridolin

You succeeded—in making me very frightened.

Wagner

(Looking at Sulphurine) Ah!—Yes, yes, the work is accomplished—There's my slave—look—

Fridolin

It's true!

Wagner

Did I make a male or did I make a female?

Fridolin

The devil! I don't know. (Going to Sulphurine who pushes him away with force) Oh!—What a fist! It's a man, Master!

Wagner

A man—! (Looking at her closely) Why no—you don't know anything about it! She's a woman! A real woman!—Slave! My pretty slave! (Sulphurine looks at him in astonishment without replying) Ah! I've created a woman—marvelous—she's not talking.

Fridolin

She doesn't talk. You are then mute, say, Madame.

Sulphurine

(Coming closer) No—what do you want with me?

Wagner

She speaks!

Fridolin

Ah! She's not as perfect as you said.

Sulphurine

Who pulled me from our world?

Wagner

Who? Why me—me—my slave.

Fridolin

We—it was us—slave.

Sulphurine

Who brought me here? What are these objects that surround me? (She touches Wagner and Fridolin) What's this?

Wagner

These are men, my slave.

Fridolin

Good-looking men.

Sulphurine

Villainous men. (Going to the window)

Fridolin

What! Who's villainous?

Wagner

She doesn't know anything yet—I will form her taste.

Sulphurine

Ah! I want to go down there!

Wagner

I will take you there, my slave.

Sulphurine

Escort me.

Wagner

I will take you there much later. I want to contemplate you, admire my work—I want—

Sulphurine

(Forcefully) Escort me right now! Instantly!

Wagner

But—

Sulphurine

(Imperiously) I wish it!

Wagner

I obey—I obey, my slave. (To Fridolin who laughs) Useless for you to laugh—I am a greater savant than Master Faustus. It is I who created this woman.

Sulphurine

(With rage) Hurry up! I'm waiting.

Wagner

At your orders, my slave. (He leaves, dragged by Sulphurine)

Fridolin

(Following them) Great savant! Great savant! I was the one who blew the fire! (He disappears by the right)

CURTAIN

SCENE II

A public place.

To the left, a church—to the right near the audience a tavern. Mephistopheles appears from a trap. Townsfolk, students, young girls, soldiers, beggars strollers going in every direction.

A Worker

Hey! The rest of you—! Where are you going?

Another

To a hunt—and you?

First Worker

We are going by the mill. (They disappear)

First Young Girl

I'm going home.

Another Girl

Come with me. We will find him outside the town, under the big poplars.

First Young Girl

Your lover? Fine pleasure for me—he will pay you court and dance with you alone.

First Student

Let's follow the pretty girls. (Indicating two other young girls passing) Now there are two others who please me more. (Sulphurine appears dressed like a country girl. She is pursued by Mephistopheles dressed as a student)

Mephistopheles

Sulphurine! Why are you running off like this?

Sulphurine

Because you are pursuing me—why are you pursuing me?

Mephistopheles

Because I find you pretty.

Sulphurine

Pretty! That's the first time they've said that word to me. They never said it to me—neither after I came to earth, nor down there, in our world.

Mephistopheles

Because down there you don't resemble what you are here.

Sulphurine

Truly?

Mephistopheles

I evoked you from our empire, so that you would come animate the body created by this Wagner. I thought you would have the appearance and outer form of a monster.

Sulphurine

Yes, but however simple, however naïve a man may be, he has a particle of the divine essence, and what he dreams, what he engenders is still a reflection of a powerful master.

Mephistopheles

It's true!

Sulphurine

Then—decidedly—I am pretty.

Mephistopheles

Charming! Adorable! And your appearance refocuses me; let me look at you.

Sulphurine

That pleases me that you are speaking to me this way—speak to me again, speak.

Mephistopheles

Yes, yes, the voice charms me and your look intoxicates me, everything about you attracts me and fascinates me, to the degree that, of itself, my hand presses yours, my arm surrounds your waist and my lips seek your lips. (He kisses her. They both let out a cry of sorrow)

Sulphurine

Ah! It's a fire that burns.

Mephistopheles

It's a poison which shreds. All my being quivers with sorrow.

Sulphurine

Fools that we are—we are dreaming of love.

Mephistopheles

Love is a divine fruit. God reserved it for his blessed creatures.—And the jealous master forbids the damned to gather it.

Sulphurine

It's true, he punished us, one after another for having for a single instant disregarded his law.

Mephistopheles

(To himself) And he is the All-Powerful—and we must bend our heads before him—Well, let men in their turn bend before us—let the wisest of them forswear his cult and his faith.

Sulphurine

Can I second you?

Mephistopheles

Yes, but it's not you that I will first confront this old geezer with.

Sulphurine

Who will it be them?

Mephistopheles

Marguerite—

Sulphurine

Marguerite! Purity, Candor, Innocence!

Mephistopheles

She will better than you catch the soul of the old sage—I've prepared the mind of the young girl—A thought that I sent her has already made her heart beat.

Sulphurine

For this old geezer?

Mephistopheles

Or at least for what he was for many years. When it leaves from her mouth, we shall see if Master Faust won't demand youth from me. (Enter Wagner and Fridolin)

Wagner

What has become of my slave?

Fridolin

Ah! There she is, Master Wagner, your slave.

Mephistopheles

His slave! It's of you he speaks?

Sulphurine

Yes; he thinks himself my Master.

Wagner

What are you doing here, my slave?

Fridolin

And in the company of a young man.

Sulphurine

(To Wagner) What's it to you? Did you create me so I would always obey you?

Wagner

Why yes! Why yes!

Mephistopheles

You are more demanding than the Divine Creator himself,

Master Wagner.

Wagner

This one knows me—And in what am I more exacting than—

Mephistopheles

God left free will to his creature—God said to man: be free.

Fridolin

Allow me, allow me—to man, yes; but not to woman.

Sulphurine

Ah!

Wagner

And I don't think I am mistaken. It was a woman I had the intention of creating.

Sulphurine

So what?

Wagner

So what? You are my work, my dear, and I order you not to play the coquette with students—ah!

Fridolin

Very fine!

Sulphurine

(Furious) You order me?

Fridolin

(Low to Wagner) Go on—be firm!

Wagner

(Hesitating low) Don't worry. (Aloud) Yes—I—I—

Sulphurine

(Wrathfully) Again!

Wagner

(Hesitating) Meaning—when I say it—I mean—What is it I was saying?

Fridolin

He's giving in—he's giving in—he is lost!

Sulphurine

You were saying—that you order me—

Wagner

Well, no—I beg you, Sulphurine—I beg you—Then!

Sulphurine

That's still too much—

Fridolin

Then?

Wagner

Well, I supplicate you, then—I conjure you, then (Mephistopheles gives Sulphurine a sign)

Sulphurine

(Crossing to the left) Go sit down over there!

Fridolin

(Imperiously) Go down there!

Wagner

(Very softly) Yes, my slave. (He goes to sit) What a funny slave I gave myself.

Fridolin

Ah! I think you have really done ill to wait upon her—your slave.

Mephistopheles

Hey! Friend.

Wagner

(With rage) What is it you want of me?

Mephistopheles

Go into that tavern and ask for some wine.

Fridolin

Ah! Fine! Are you going to serve this one, too?

Wagner

(Rising, furious) For you—I don't wish—

Sulphurine

But as for me, I wish it—

Wagner

In that case—

Fridolin

Resist, will you—

Wagner

Yes, I'm resisting—Go in there, Fridolin.

Fridolin

And they call this a man.

Sulphurine

(Impatiently to Fridolin) Get going!

Fridolin

Who's (astonished) that?

Sulphurine

Why, you!

Fridolin

What! You want me—

Sulphurine

Why, certainly—

Fridolin

(Naively) Well, yes, I am going (He goes into the tavern)

Wagner

And to think I'd put a whole sheep into the pot. (He goes to the left watching Mephistopheles, who sits at the table)

Mephistopheles

(To Sulphurine) I was speaking to you before the arrival of Wagner—

Sulphurine

Of the one you want to ruin.

Fridolin

(Reappearing) They refuse to sell wine during the hours of the church service.

Sulphurine

(To Mephistopheles) Here's Marguerite. (At this moment Marguerite appears in the door of the church)

Mephistopheles

And Faustus—I will make them ruin each other, and I will have two souls instead of one. Wait (They go down right)

Faust

I've arrived too late; the divine office is terminated.

Sulphurine

(Aside) What's he going to do?

Mephistopheles

(Approaching Marguerite) On my soul, I've never seen a man charming child.

Marguerite

What do you want of me?

Mephistopheles

A kiss.

Marguerite

A kiss—I refuse.

Mephistopheles

And as for me, I'm taking it (He wants to take her by the waist. She seeks refuge by Faust)

Marguerite

Protect me, Milord.

Faust

The beautiful young girl—(To Mephistopheles) Go—get back—

Mephistopheles

Respect to the learned doctor. Pardon—my beauty (He bows) (To himself) Marvelous—they are in a fine way! (Making a sign for Sulphurine to follow him)

Wagner

Fridolin, let's not leave her in the power of that man (They disappear)

Marguerite

Thanks for your protection.

Faust

I rid you of the gallantries of a student—I don't deserve great gratitude.

Marguerite

That one had something evil in his look which shook my heart.

Faust

He terrified you?

Marguerite

Yes. You on the contrary have a benevolent air, I am completely reassured—Thanks and goodbye! (She moves away to the right)

Faust

Why leave me so fast, since I don't frighten you?

Marguerite

(Stopping) Have you something to tell me?

Faust

(After a pause) Yes.

Marguerite

In that case, speak.

Faust

What's your name?

Marguerite

Marguerite—

Faust

And who are your parents?

Marguerite

I have only a mother—who's waiting for me—

Faust

Are you in a hurry?

Marguerite

Yes, our household is quite small, and yet it is necessary to take care of it—we don't have a serving girl.

Faust

No serving girl—

Marguerite

Oh! We are not poor! My father left us a little house with a garden when he died. My brother Valentin is a soldier; he's serving in Italy, in Calabria—My little sister is dead, my mother has only me about her—and I tried to avoid tiring her. From the moment the Sun rises, it's necessary to be at the wash house, then the market, then cares of the house, and every day like that—It's a lot of work, but sleep that follows seems only more sweet, and one dozes off at night, blessing the Lord who gave us rest and bread each day.

Faust

Marguerite—you are an angel.

Marguerite

I am only a poor child—whose language must make you smile with pity.

Faust

Marguerite there's something in the purity of your glance, in the chaste beauty of your face an irresistibly compelling charm. God seems to have joined in you alone, all the most precious gifts. You appear and one admires you; you appear and one loves you—(During this speech Marguerite has listened but placed her hands over her face)

Marguerite

Oh! Continue! Continue forever!

Faust

Why are you hiding your face?

Marguerite

Because all you are telling me, I seem to have heard it already—in a dream.

Faust

A dream!

Marguerite

And I was closing my eyes to find the features of the one who spoke to me that way. I wasn't able to find his features, the voice was the same.

Faust

The voice? It was my voice you heard?

Marguerite

It was even your eyes—calm and kind—Ah!—I can almost see him again.

Faust

In that case he resembled me?

Marguerite

Yes, he resembled you.

Faust

Could it be joyfully?

Marguerite

But he was a young man.

Faust

(Sadly) A young man!

Marguerite

Do you have a son?

Faust

(Sorrowfully) A son?

Marguerite

He's the one I must have met—whose memory visited my sleep.

Faust

I was mad! I was forgetting my years, my wrinkles and my grey hair. (Escorting her away) Goodbye, Marguerite, goodbye!

Marguerite

Goodbye! You have a son, right?

Faust

Goodbye! (She leaves by the right) (Alone) A son! She would love me if I were young!

Mephistopheles

(Reappearing) Order, Master—

Faust

(Who didn't see him, turning) You—will—so be it!—I want youth!

Mephistopheles

Youth and love—follow me.

Faust

Where to?

Mephistopheles

Out of town where we will attend the ancient sorceress of Thessaly. Come.

Faust

Let's go! (They leave)

CURTAIN

SCENE III

The Ruins.

In the midst is a large cauldron, under it a very bright fire. The stage is dimly lit. An invisible choir is heard.

Sulphurine dressed as a sorceress appears; the action takes place during the chorus that follows. She indicates to one who has a distaff to spin; and another with a box of herbs in front of her to prepare it.

Chorus

The horned crescent
Over bald mountain
Is rising!
One would say the iron
Of a sword
Is being forged by hell

(After this chorus, great hubbub amongst the sorceress, who vanish at the entry of Wagner and Fridolin)

Fridolin

(Following Wagner) What are we coming to do here, Master Wagner?

Wagner

(With anger) What do you mean why are we coming—it's my slave Sulphurine who seemed to want it—I don't know why.

Fridolin

(With apprehension) I am not at all comfortable here—and you, Master Wagner—are you afraid?

Wagner

Me! I'm never afraid (Two white ghosts slip across the ruins to the right)

Fridolin

You are really lucky.

Wagner

(Looking at the ghosts and speaking with emotion) No—I'm never—I'm—What was that! And—and you—Fridolin—do you—are you afraid sometimes?

Fridolin

Always, Master.

Wagner

(Seeing three ghosts pass) Oh!

Fridolin

(Trembling) Hah?

Wagner

It's terrifying.

Fridolin

(Holding him lightly) What?

Wagner

It's horrible—lo'...look—

Fridolin

Not—not at all—if it's horrible I don't want to look—But you, who are never afraid—it seems to me you are trembling a lot—

Wagner

I'm not afraid; but I—I am very nervous. (Several more ghosts enter)

Fridolin

(Looking at the left) Master!—Master!

Wagner

(Looking at the right) Fri...Fridolin.

Fridolin

There—there—on the right.

Wagner

There—there—on the left.

Sulphurine

(Who's come up behind them, tapping them on the shoulder) Silence! Who's making so much noise in my place?

Wagner

Your—your place—who then are you, Madam?—

Sulphurine

The mistress of this place.

Fridolin

Ah! You are—the—you have a villainous domicile.

Wagner

And you have a terrible way of announcing yourself—you almost frightened us—

Fridolin

Ah, yes—you really almost—

Sulphurine

You are two cowards—I know you—

Wagner

Ah! You know—In that case, my kind lady, could you inform me what we've come to do in these ruins—

Sulphurine

You've been sent her to be useful to your Master, the savant, Doctor Faustus.

Fridolin

But respectable lady—in what way can we be of service to Doctor Faust?

Sulphurine

He's coming here for me to rid him of the heavy burden of his years.

Fridolin

He wants to be rejuvenated.

Sulphurine

Yes—

Wagner

And it's possible to perform this miracle?

Sulphurine

Nothing is impossible to science, but time never abdicates its rights; and the years removed from Faust must weigh on the head of another man.

Wagner

I pity the another one—And who will the unfortunate be?

Sulphurine

(Low) Who?—there are two of you here.

Fridolin

Who will be the unfortunate who will inherit from...?

Sulphurine

(Low) You didn't come alone.

Fridolin

(Looking at Wagner) Ah!

Wagner

(Aside) This poor Fridolin!

Fridolin

(Aside) This poor Wagner!

Sulphurine

Now to work. (She waves a distaff. Monkeys and cats surround her)

Wagner

What are all these horrible animals?

Sulphurine

They are my guests.

Fridolin

Your guests? You rescue very villainous company—

Sulphurine

For the spell, I need a fire of box wood and holly. (To Wagner) Go find me the necessary wood.

Wagner

Instantly—Come, Fridolin, come my poor Fridolin.

Fridolin

Yes, yes—Master Wagner.

Wagner

My friend, these are the very perishable treasures of youth and a pretty face.

Fridolin

A beautiful soul is worth more than some charms.

Wagner

(Aside) He seems to be prepared for the thing.

Fridolin

(Aside) I think this won't cause him too much despair.

Wagner

(To Fridolin) Let's go, come! (he takes him by the arm and they disappear)

Sulphurine

Come on, children, to work! The Master's going to come! (General movement—Then during the chorus that follows she throws the herbs into the fire. Another sorcerer shakes the contents.)

Chorus

Despite the grumbling
Quick to work!
Blood from the vein
All hot
Must
Mix with verbena
Stir, stir fast
And in the cauldron
Pour
The frozen
Tears and laughter
Of pale vampires!
The horned crescent
Is rising

Over bald mountain
One would say the steel
Of a sword
In being forged in hell

Mephistopheles

(At the back) This way, Master Faust. (General movement—Mephistopheles descends toward the center of the stage. The monkeys and cats come to roll at his feet then go back to place themselves around the cauldron)

Faust

(Coming forward) I'm here! (All bow to him) Where are we? (Looking around him) Ruins?

Mephistopheles

It's the hide out of my old friend (To Sulphurine) Greetings, Gertrude.

Faust

(To Mephistopheles) Cannot you yourself prepare this brew?

Mephistopheles

It takes many years for that, much art and patience, the devil has no time to waste—come sorceress, my sweet—

Sulphurine

Master, I am awaiting your orders.

Mephistopheles

Trace around Faustus the circle of the great Paracelsus, pronounce the cabalistic words, and present him with a full cup of your elixir.

Sulphurine

Come to me, Faust.

Faust

I'm here! (Goes to mid stage)

Chorus

By the three teeth
Of the red dragon
With burning eyes
And by the hovel
Of Old Gerfaut
Where Empousse
The terrible spouse
Of the scaffold;
By the torture
Plaintive lover
Of dark winters
By the green eyes
Of Godly Vertigo
By misfortune
By the humble stein
Of flowering stubble
By the shadows
The funereal veils
Of Circe
To the frozen breast

Of Mercy
By science
By power
King of somber places (Forcefully)
By a hundred trumpets (Forcefully)
Prince of shades (Forcefully)
We adjure you (Forcefully)
We adjure you!
We adjure you!

(She offers the cup to Faust—at the moment he places it to his lips a light flame rises—Faust stops speechless)

Mephistopheles

Well! What's stopping you? You intend to drive off the fire of age and you recoil before the fire of youth? Are you afraid, Faustus?

Faust

Whether this cup contains life or death, I will empty it with a single gulp.

CURTAIN

SCENE IV

The Enchanted Gardens.

The ruins have been replaced by enchanted gardens. The sorceresses have changed into nymphs. Everywhere youth and springtime, and Faust rejuvenated like all that surrounds him is strolling delighted. Wagner and Fridolin are suddenly old.

Sulphurine

See, Faust, everything here is rejuvenated with you.

Wagner

(At the left) Rejuvenated—is he lucky?

Fridolin

(At the right) There he is, young and lucky like us.

Faust

(Looking in a mirror that a nymph presents to him) Is it really me? Is it indeed my blood that's boiling this way in my veins? This powerful life which seems to give me wings—is it really my life? My life, just now trembling and bent, and now standing straight, energetic and young! Is it my life which strips off the mountain of ice that covered it, or is this really the world, nature, the ages which have turned back on their path? I greet you, o earth which breathes all revivified under my feet. Earth, earth you have reconquered me! I salute you! I love you. (Contemplating the groups of nymphs) Who are these groups of young and beautiful women who are surrounding me? Oh! All the remains of age in my heart I can feel, melting under their glances.

Chorus

We are the perfume of roses
We are the breezes of May
Flee, flee morose spirits
The bird is singing its virelay

(Dances)

Mephistopheles

Listen, Faustus, here are the precious gifts I am offering you—

Sulphurine

(To Faust, indicating to him a nymph who holds a rich coffer filled with gold)

Of your youth
Let all be reborn,
Hopes, dreams and harvest
When all rush
Towards opulence
Listen to the jingling song of gold

Chorus

We are the perfume of roses—(Dances)

Sulphurine

(Now indicating a nymph who presents a basket of fruit and vine branches)

The Sun brightens
What I adore
I am the spirit of green vines
The mad orgy
Of red wine
Laughingly defies me perverse gods

Chorus

We are the perfume of roses

(Dances)

Sulphurine

(Indicating a nymph who holds a basket of flowers)

Ardent or languishing
For us
The rose has never withered
Come, our intoxication
Charms and caresses;
Come, in our eyes imbibe forgetfulness

Chorus

We are, etc, (Dances)

Sulphurine

Sensuality for you!

Faust

No, no, it is not sensuality, it's love that I want—Marguerite, my rediscovered life belongs to you completely—(In response an immense outburst of laughter)

Mephistopheles

Love—Ha! Ha! Ha! (Faust rushes toward the back)

Wagner

Let's follow Master Faust, Fridolin.

Fridolin

And mix our youth with his. (They meet and look at each other)

Wagner

Ah! My God.

Fridolin

Ah! Heaven! It's you who have inherited.

Wagner

What, my poor Fridolin—it's you who have—

Sulphurine

(Giving them each a mirror) You are sharing in it as good friends.

Wagner

I've lost my freshness, the lilies of my complexion, and the roses of my cheeks—

Fridolin

I've lost my beauty! Alas! Poor withered flower—I have nothing else but to die. (Faust reappears. He makes a sign of command to Mephistopheles)

Mephistopheles

Where are we going, Master?

Faust

To Marguerite.

Chorus of Spirits and Nymphs

Ha, ha, ha, ha, ha, ha, ha!
To our fevers you prefer
The cup of pure frolics
Ha, ha, ha, ha, ha, ha, ha!
But there's more than one false step
Twixt that cup and your lips!
Ha, ha, ha, ha, ha, ha, ha!

CURTAIN

SCENE V

Marguerite's garden.

To the left, Marguerite's house. Entrance door facing the audience. On the street floor, in cutaway a window, another on the next floor. Near the house—a table. At the back and to the right a very shady garden. In the foreground a bench.

Marguerite is in the street floor window seated dozing leaning on the window. Mephistopheles and Sulphurine in country costume enter quietly from the right.

Mephistopheles

I've made you take the place of her neighbor, Martha, so you can distract the mind of the young girl.

Sulphurine

Why did you choose me and not Faust himself?

Mephistopheles

Because woman has remained, since the day of creation, the premier temptress in the world.

Sulphurine

Oh! The first was the serpent, you know that better than anyone.

Mephistopheles

Yes, but the pupil profited so well by the lesson that the Master can be put in retirement! Women now possess the art of seduction, of deceiving, of ruining. That's why, in our times serpents no longer speak.

Sulphurine

How will I tempt Marguerite?

Mephistopheles

Here, here's wherewith to fascinate her eyes and her mind. (Gives her a box)

Sulphurine

(Opening the box) Oh! Magnificent jewels!

Mephistopheles

She's going to awaken! I'm escaping, remember!—(He disappears)

Marguerite

(Opening her eyes and noticing Sulphurine, who seems absorbed in the contemplation of jewels) What are you doing there, neighbor?

Sulphurine

Admiring—and I envy you.

Marguerite

Envy me?

Sulphurine

Yes, since it's for you that they just brought this rich present.

Marguerite

A present! For me? (She disappears from the window)

Sulphurine

She's coming. You will be obeyed, my Master.

Marguerite

(Emerging from the house) Let's see! How these jewels—this ornament which would honor a great lady in feast days?

Sulphurine

A handsome cavalier ordered me to give them to you on his behalf.

Marguerite

But I must not accept.

Sulphurine

Why? He is so rich that in his eyes it seems to be an object of little value. He begged me, with so many entreaties to offer them to you—that you will make him very unhappy, I believe, by not accepting them. See how they will go with you.

Marguerite

No.

Sulphurine

Let me do it—nothing wrong with trying them on— (She puts the jewels on her) Oh! How pretty you are like that!

Marguerite

You find it so? Poor as I am, I would never dare to go with this get-up either on a stroll or to church! And then what would my mother say?

Sulphurine

Good, I'll take care of everything. First you will put on a little chain, then a diamond, then a pearl, little by little you will be dressed in rich jewels, and as for your mother—trust me, I will invent something.

Marguerite

But this cavalier, what will he think?

Sulphurine

That you are not very offended by his love.

Marguerite

His love! I don't want it (She pushes away the jewels) (Mephistopheles and Faust enter)

Sulphurine

Here he is.

Marguerite

(Recognizing Faust and uttering a weak scream) Ah!

Faust

(Going to Marguerite) Is it my presence that troubles you this way, child?

Marguerite

Yes.

Faust

Why?

Marguerite

(Aside) Oh! My dream, my beautiful dream.

Mephistopheles

(Aside) Remembering the dream I sent her.

Faust

Well?

Marguerite

Yesterday I met an old man who resembles you.

Faust

Well, that old man was—

Mephistopheles

It was his father, and I wager you turned the head of the old savant as much as his son. (He approaches Marguerite who moves away swiftly)

Faust

Eh! But—what's wrong with you, beautiful?

Marguerite

(Pointing to Mephistopheles) That's—your friend?

Faust

My—companion.

Marguerite

He frightens me.

Mephistopheles

Fright! Ha, ha, ha! (Laughing)

Marguerite

(Low to Faust) His presence makes me ill. I experience horror looking at him.

Faust

Child—

Marguerite

His eyes are nasty and mocking. He seems to wear, written on his face, that his soul can love no other soul.

Faust

(Low) An angel's forebodings (To Mephistopheles) Distance yourself.

Mephistopheles

I obey, Master—quite soon, I will be useless here. Love is between you two; it will do the devil's work. (Faust takes Marguerite's arm and strolls with her)

Marguerite

(Watching Mephistopheles move away) Ah! I am breathing now—

Faust

Well, let's chat, do you want to?

Marguerite

So it was actually your father who protected, defended me?

Faust

Yesterday, leaving the church, yes—and it's because he spoke to me at length of this meeting that I wanted to see you; I was seeking you throughout the whole town, and I'm really lucky to have found you.

Marguerite

Why?

Faust

Because my father's words gave birth in my heart to a sentiment previously unknown.

Marguerite

In that case, what did he say to you?

Faust

First of all, he told me of your adorable grace.

Marguerite

Him!

Faust

Of your charming figure, of your hands so delicate and white—delightful hands. (He kisses them) Then he spoke to me of the golden tresses of your hair.

Marguerite

But he only saw me for a moment.

Faust

And that moment sufficed for him to admire the purity of your look, the sweetness of your voice; he spoke to me of your naïve candor and the ingenuousness of your soul.

Marguerite

Here I am all confused—

Faust

Why?

Marguerite

He spoke to you of so many things you aren't going to find in me.

Faust

To the contrary, it seems to me that his weak eyes saw ill, ill understood what I am now admiring. Marguerite, if your beauty, was able to move the heart of an old geezer, with what trouble will you fill a soul that age has not frozen!—With what fire will it embrace my heart whose first love you are!

Marguerite

You love me, you say—? But you hardly know me!

Faust

What does it matter that today be the day I found you, if you are for so long the object of my dreams? Marguerite, I've desired you for a long time that I've called you; it's a long time that I've loved you! (He takes her in his arms)

Marguerite

My God! I don't understand what's taking place inside me, all that he's saying to me fills me at the same time with joy and fear—His words make my heart beat sweetly , and I tremble as I listen to him—and—I don't dare glance at him—I am happy near him (Disengaging) and I want to distance myself—what is this that I am experiencing? (To Faust, looking at him timidly) I think that I am a little crazy.

Faust

No, no, you are an angel and I love you (A burst of laughter from Mephistopheles is heard)

Marguerite

(Uttering a cry of terror) Ah! My God! That laughter.

Faust

It's nothing, it's my companion, who, no question, is jesting with your friend.

Marguerite

(Sitting at the right) I was afraid!

Faust

Calm down! Calm down!

Marguerite

Oh! It's that no one has ever spoken to me as you did. What do you want? I am only a poor child, very simple and ignorant. You are not seeking to deceive me, are you?

Faust

I love you, Marguerite, I love you.

Marguerite

For true? Wait (She detaches a Marguerite that she has in her belt and strips it of its petals) He loves me!—He loves me not!—Yes—No—(Joyfully) He loves me!

Faust

Marguerite! (He takes her in his arms and embraces her)

Marguerite

(Escaping) Ah! I'm afraid! I'm afraid!

Faust

Listen to me.

Marguerite

(Troubled) It's late, here's evening. Good night (To Sulphurine) Good night (To Faust) Good night.

Mephistopheles

Already!

Sulphurine

Couldn't we go in your place?

Marguerite

Receive so much company—what would my mother say? (To Faust) Till tomorrow.

Faust

Tomorrow.

Mephistopheles

Tomorrow is so long.

Faust

A century without seeing you—I have so many things to tell you—I wouldn't like to leave you for an hour, for a minute; I would live and die near you—why refuse to receive me?

Marguerite

And my mother who locks all the doors?

Mephistopheles

God, he knows how to get through the window—a light placed in front of the transept can serve as a signal and light the way—that's the advice I give you.

Marguerite

It must be bad—(To Faust) Good night.

Faust

I'll wait for the signal.

Marguerite

No—no—good night—good night (She disappears—at a sign from Mephistopheles, Sulphurine goes out as well)

Mephistopheles

Bravo, Master—I found you superb—

Faust

What do you mean?

Mephistopheles

In seduction.

Faust

This is not seduction—it's love—

Mephistopheles

Of what love are we speaking? I knew five or six of 'em who are my friends.

Faust

The one I feel for Marguerite is a chaste, pure, divine love! You are unaware of that; men alone experience it.

Mephistopheles

By reputation—it's possible. Indeed, she's a charming mistress, Marguerite.

Faust

A mistress! Ah, that's your fist snare. (Laughing) Poor and clumsy demon! A mistress—She will be the companion of my whole life—she will be my life.

Mephistopheles

In that case, it's a break-up—you are sending me away?

Faust

Why, yes—

Mephistopheles

Ah! Ah!—I understand, a wife, little children, who will form around the pious doctor a blessed cordon of prayers and canticles! A wife and children! Meaning the joys of the foyer and celestial blessings!

Faust

Why not?

Mephistopheles

(To himself) Oh—not at all, Master, not at all.

Faust

(Who has gone under Marguerite's window) What are you thinking about?

Mephistopheles

Why, doctor, I was offering you a love of some weeks, of happiness for a season—and here you are thinking of chaining yourself up all your life—That was really worth the trouble of making time march backwards to your profit! Ah, Master, follow my advice, taste all sorts of loves, all sorts of happiness.

Faust

No!

Mephistopheles

Come with me to Italy, the country of dark, passionate, coquettish women—! To England, the nation of blonde women—! To France, the country of blondes and brunettes, passionate, sentimental and coquettish women—

Faust

I would have been able to follow you if Marguerite, less chaste and less pure, had granted me just now, the rendezvous you requested for me.

Mephistopheles

Ah! (Extending his arm) So, were she to receive you this evening, were she to give the signal?

Faust

And I will follow you tomorrow. (At a gesture from Mephistopheles, a light is placed in Marguerite's window)

Mephistopheles

Look—your beauty is awaiting you (Pointing to the light)

Faust

Marguerite!

Mephistopheles

(Aside) Thanks, my will o' the wisp.

Faust

Marguerite!

Mephistopheles

The signal, there it is. (The table changes into a ladder and raises itself right up to Marguerite's window) Goodness! Here's the way.

Faust

(After an interior struggle) Come on! She's beautiful, I'm young, and I love her—(He rushes to the ladder, climbs it and vanishes through the window)

Mephistopheles

(Aside) You will follow me tomorrow?

Sulphurine

(Reappearing) Well, Master?

Mephistopheles

(Pointing to the window) He is there!

Sulphurine

There!

Mephistopheles

Yes, there, with her! Today love, tomorrow jealousy, soon crime! It's now I have need of you.

Sulphurine

What must be done?

Mephistopheles

Be beautiful, be a woman, and remember that you are the daughter of hell!

Sulphurine

I will remember, Master. (They vanish)

CURTAIN

SCENE VI

In church.

The exterior porch of the church is on the left. The stage is dimly lit. (Marguerite and several young girls)

Sybille

The evening office has not yet begun. (Opens one of the church doors)

Gudulle

Speak low...nonetheless, it's not suitable to raise your voice near the house of God.

Sybille

(To Lisette) Ah! There you are, Lisette—do you know the news?

Lisette

No—

Sybille

And you, Marguerite?

Marguerite

(Sad and distracted) What news?

Sybille

Little Barbara—haven't you heard tell of her?

Marguerite

I see little of the world.

Sybille

Well, she too has ended by turning bad—

Marguerite

(Shivering) Ah! She, too!

Gudulle

It really ought to have been foreseen.

Sybille

Yes—There they were with all their grand airs. My God, it was a long while that she was hanging around after that wiseacre. First of all it was pure gallantry—Then came the rendezvous—The words of love.

Marguerite

(Dolefully) Ah!

Gudulle

So many there were that in the end wise girls can do nothing but turn away from her—and as a sign of shame cast broken straw in front of her door.

Marguerite

Poor girl!

Sybille

(Going to her) You pity her, Marguerite—What's become of your virtuous principles?

Marguerite

Who knows how the unfortunate succumbed?

Lisette

Marguerite's right. Sybille, you are strict for a poor fallen girl.

Sybille

It's that I know too well what to beware of—

Gudulle

That's true—you listen to the sweet talk from vanity at first—then your heart is seized, virtue dozes, and when you awake you find yourself alone, abandoned by the one you thought loved you—and with abandonment comes discouragement, misery, and shame—(The organ is heard) Come to pray, sisters. (They go into the church)

Marguerite

(Alone, bursting into tears and falling on her knees) Yes, it's always thus that it ends—always! Oh celestial mother!—cast a glance of pity on me—! Alas!—The sweet peace of my life is no more—who will understand the hurt that shreds my soul and the bitter suffering I drag with me—! Save me from shame and death o celestial mother, I am weeping, I am weeping. (She remains supplicating and overcome)

Mephistopheles

(Appearing suddenly and looking at Marguerite) In the depth of Italy, a perfume of repentance came to strike me in the face! I shivered, and for a moment I abandoned Faust at grips with the most beautiful and clever courtesans of Naples! With the beat of a wing I crossed the distance. It was indeed Marguerite who was praying. The struggle is here now. There—on that stone where the fallen angel weeps. Ah! Wounded injured dove, you are still protected by celestial legions, but, I too, I am called legion! (He approaches Marguerite and envelops her with his looks)

Marguerite

(Rising) Where's it come from—to obtain the pardon I implore—where's the cause that I cannot even pray anymore? Good God!—it's a divine word—!

Mephistopheles

You won't say it.

Marguerite

What's wrong with me? I feel myself trembling still, I'm shivering! And I cannot find one word; I cannot find one tear to express the repentance of my soul.

Mephistopheles

Let her succumb and let her die of shock before that repentance reaches God. (The first measures of a funeral chant are heard)

Funeral Chant

Day of honor and wrath
You shine like a lightning burst on sin
And strike the most hidden crime
Where will I find refuge?
O my father, o my judge
Save me from this abyss!

Marguerite

(Rising, shocked) That funeral chant—it's for me—it's—O Lord! Lord I wish to pray—I wish—(She falls on her knees)

Mephistopheles

(Low) You won't pray.

Marguerite

Ah! I'm ill—I'm ill.

Mephistopheles

Marguerite!

Marguerite

(Rising terrified) Ah! Who's calling me (Turning towards Mephistopheles who remains invisible to her)

Mephistopheles

(Low) Your eyes won't see me.

Marguerite

No one! Is this the voice of my conscience?

Mephistopheles

Yes, it's crying to you. Don't seek peace anymore, renounce all hope—God himself has turned his glance from you.

Marguerite

Then there's no more salvation?

Mephistopheles

Nothing more for you but misfortune.

Marguerite

Ah! I am lost! I am lost!

Mephistopheles

Tell me—what's become of the innocence of your soul? What's become of the virtue so proud, without pity for those who fell? You who know so well how to recognize those who don't tread. The Lord's path, those who bear on their brow the sign of the curse, descend to the bottom of your heart and pronounce judgment on yourself.

Marguerite

Oh! That voice—that voice which screams from the depths of my breast.

Mephistopheles

Your breast, modest virgin, aren't you already feeling grow the fruit of your shame?

Marguerite

(Uttering a cry) Ah! (She places a hand on her heart and remains staring fixedly) (The funeral chant is heard more loudly)

Mephistopheles

Hark! The wrath of God is breaking over you, the trumpet is sounding, the tombs are shaking and the ashes of your body, reanimated by eternal flames, shiver with terror. (She rises) Listen, the sepulchre shook—it's the sepulchre where your crime will drive your mother.

Marguerite

Mother! Mother! (Funeral chant) What shocking anguish—! That terrible chant is destroying me!

Mephistopheles

It's the funeral song of your brother. Your shame will kill him.

Marguerite

Ah! Air! Air!

Mephistopheles

Air! Light! Hide yourself, wretch—but shame and crime cannot hide. Bad luck to you—bad luck!

Marguerite

Ah! Help! Help—(She falls in a faint)

Mephistopheles

Come, I've got my prey—to the other one now (He disappears. The young girls come out of church, hurry to raise her then lead her away, supporting her)

CURTAIN

SCENE VII

Resina.

A vine arbor.

Fridolin

How happy I am, Master Wagner.

Wagner

Truly, my Lad? And what are you happy about?

Fridolin

Why, first of all for becoming young again, which allows me to taste the charm of this ravishing climate.

Wagner

Yes, yes, I understand.

Fridolin

For—it has to be said—here we are become—

Wagner

Young and charming as before.

Fridolin

But who performed this miracle?

Wagner

Who? Me!

Fridolin

You?

Wagner

(With scorn) With the aid of the sorceress—there are mysteries of high science you cannot appreciate.

Fridolin

Ah!

Wagner

The honest sorceress at the prayer of Master Faust—and on mine—was pleased to exact the prayers of some of those imbeciles who repeat at every moment "Ah! What would I then be tomorrow—Ah—what would I be a month from now—Ah, what would I be a year later"—And she took from us one day, one month, one year to give them.

Fridolin

Very fine—she took that on your head and on mine.

Wagner

And if she had wanted to satisfy the whole world, we would quite soon be back nursing.

Fridolin

She stopped in time— As for me, I feel very well.

Wagner

Me, too.

Fridolin

And here we are in beautiful Italy.

Wagner

In Naples, or at least very near Naples—in Resina—I've long had the intention of visiting this magnificent country, and as my slave had exactly the same desire—I have done it—

Fridolin

Huh—

Wagner

She—

Fridolin

Yes—

Wagner

Anyway, we came here—

Fridolin

Ah! She's really obedient—really obedient, your slave!

Wagner

Yes, isn't she?

Fridolin

Hold on, Master Wagner, between ourselves, I think we've been tricked.

Wagner

What?

Fridolin

By the sheep vendor.

Wagner

Sheep? What sheep vendor?

Fridolin

The man with the lambs.

Wagner

Lambs! Ah, good.

Fridolin

There are moments when I ask myself if the animal we put in the cauldron wasn't rather a savage little wild cat.

Wagner

A wild cat? You're crazy. Sulphurine is adorable and I think in my heart I'm going to resemble that ancient sculptor—Pygmalion.

Fridolin

Pygmalion?

Wagner

Who fell in love with his statue.

Fridolin

You're in love with a statue?

Wagner

And what a statue! What marvelous beauty—all Italy is on its knees before Sulphurine.

Fridolin

Ah! Yes—That's true—Say then, tell me—why did she change her name?

Wagner

She calls herself Olympia—it's prettier, it's Italian, Olympia—and it's apparent I created her immensely rich.

Fridolin

Ah, bah!

Wagner

Yes, my friend, she came to the world with jewels, villa—and Faust, the famous Faust himself has become desperately in love with her. What homage rendered to my genius!

Fridolin

Ah! Yes—but for whom does that little turtledove's heart that I introduced—palpitate?

Wagner

For whom? For me—for me alone.

Fridolin

For you—?

Wagner

Yes, yes—she adores me to the degree that she cannot be without me for a single instant. When she's strolling—I am there at a distance carrying her mantle, her parasol and her little dog.

Fridolin

Fine!

Wagner

When she's dining I have to be near her—

Fridolin

Yes, behind her—

Wagner

Behind her chair—changing her napkins and filling her cup: she only eats what I present to her; she only drinks the wines I pour for her—in the end what can I say, I am her Patito, her Segisbe, her—

Fridolin

Her servant.

Wagner

Servant! Wretch! You de-poetize everything!

Fridolin

What's this outfit you're wearing?

Wagner

(Embarrassed) This?—it's a fantasy that she had—she wants me to be adorned with gold.

Fridolin

It's the dress of a servant! Come on, come on—you are the servant of your slave.

Wagner

Shut up, shut up, wretch! Have pity on my weakness—respect my illusions—you see that I adore her—(Seeing Faust enter) Ah! There's my rival.

Fridolin

(Aside) Ah, indeed! Is he that stupid, my Master?

Faust

Olympia has not yet appeared?

Fridolin

Not yet, Master.

Faust

How long it is to see her!

Wagner

My illustrious Master has then completely forgotten little Marguerite?

Faust

(With emotion) Marguerite—a child sweet and calm—whose soul is as cold as our frigid Germany—No, no, you are not she who must initiate me into the ardent passion that I've rivived—to these joys, those sorrows, those terrible struggles with love which are life.

Fridolin

And it's here, near signora Olympia, that you have found the realization of your dreams?

Faust

Yes, it's only since I've seen her that I exist! There's energy in her mind, in the strange vibration of her voice, in the somber gleam of her eyes, something which fascinates me and sweeps me away. What I experience by Olympia is vertigo, delirium, madness! Perhaps it's the air I breathe here, the embalmed air of Sorrento which intoxicates my heart—! It's the perfume of oranges in flower which intoxicates my senses! It's the sun of ancient Parthenope which reheats my soul! It's the fire of Vesuvius which makes my blood boil; it's love in the end, fiery, tyrannous love, unknown until today which distracts all my being which throws me distracted and trembling at Olympia's knees. (Movement of fury by Wagner)

Wagner

Oh! That's enough.

Faust

What's the matter?

Wagner

(Calming down) Do you know something, Signor Faust?

Faust

What?

Wagner

(Ironic) You are not the only one taken by this sovereign beauty.

Faust

You are talking of Valentin?

Wagner

(Astonished) Valentin? What, there's another one. Then we are three!

Faust

That officer of fortune—that adventurer.

Fridolin

Oh—women love adventures greatly and especially adventurers.

Faust

Does he dare to dispute Olympia with me?

Wagner

(Aside) Let's discourage him! (Aloud) He's brave—! He will dare all!

Faust

Him! We shall see!

Wagner

(To Fridolin) Jealousy! They're going to kill each other.

Fridolin

(Looking to the right) Wait—here he is.

Wagner

With my beautiful slave!

Faust

It's she—Always this Valentin!

Wagner

(With rage) Oh this Valentin.

Olympia

(Appearing) Wagner, have them prepare arm chairs for us—This place is delightful and we are going to rest here a bit. (To Wagner, who is in ecstasy) Come on, hurry up. (Wagner hurries to place seats—to Faust) Are you fleeing me, signor Faust? (To Wagner) Wagner—don't forget my orders, go!

Wagner

Yes, my slave.

Fridolin

Her orders. Ah! You see plainly that you are her servant.

Wagner

Silence, wretch—and follow me, I order you—

Fridolin

Yes, my Master. (Aside) He'll avenge himself on me, the coward.

Wagner

Huh?

Fridolin

(Bowing) Yes, my sweet Master—(They disappear to the left)

Olympia

(Holding a bouquet in her hand) I was seeking you, in truth, Lord Faust.

Faust

You have deigned to notice my absence? Yet to do that were you able to forget Captain Valentin and his words of love?

Olympia

You guessed correctly: he was in a gallant vein.

Mephistopheles

A charming gallantry.

Faust

Ah!

Valentin

I love the Signora, I say it well, if you love her, too, let's declare open and honest war!

Faust

War!

Mephistopheles

Eh! Eh! Why not? Do you think that the beautiful Olympia won't be a prize worthy of envy to the conqueror?

Olympia

Do you think that great passions or great sacrifices are offered only to irreproachable virtues and that the rest of us sinners for love must content ourselves with passing homage? Oh! We also have our adoration without limits, and better still—now, as formerly, we have our flatterers.

Mephistopheles

It's time—poets sang of ancient courtesans as they sing of them today, and writers and poets will celebrate them even in the future (Laughter) Yes, yes, I'm a bit of a sorcerer—and I foretell to you that a day will come when writers of my acquaintance will exploits the intimate life of these women; they will expose to the eyes of the world the wounds of these withered souls; they will attempt to rehabilitate them; they will disguise the shame of these lost creatures, they will guild their miseries with a touching interest, and the crowd will come to weep over their sorrows as if these sorrows were a martyrdom and not a punishment.

Valentin

Is this then such a great evil?

Olympia

Oh! It's not us who we pity for it.

Mephistopheles

Me neither.

Olympia

But virtue—what will it say?

Mephistopheles

Oh! Virtue! That's very fine. It's admired but with an eye dry and cold, and it will happen that women chaste and honest seeing so much interest, prodigal of sentimental vice, so many tears shed over it, will ask if virtue is not vice, and vice is virtue, and to attract a little of this sweet sympathy, naively distracted, they will borrow from their rivals first of all the boldness of their coquetry, then a little of their lascivious graces, then their insolent hurry, their language, even to the oddness of their manner, so well, that seeing them pass at a distance their honest husbands will ask themselves, astonished: which is my mistress?, and:

which is my wife?

Faust

You are mistaken!

Mephistopheles

Truly?

Faust

True virtue is never distracted this way, it never has either hesitation or calculation; it knows that the man who turns away from her momentarily will soon return, unalterable and strong, it has respect for itself and consciousness of its strength—Those of whom you are telling us are tottering virtues which seek danger who cry quite loud as they are being dragged to their fall and who are not troubled by falling.

Valentin

Truly, Master Faust, you do not speak like a young lover.

Olympia

It's true, you speak like an old philosopher.

Faust

(Troubled) Me! Is this the love of an old geezer I am offering you?

Olympia

No, you've committed for me all the follies of youth.

Faust

And Captain Valentin?

Valentin

Oh! As for me, I have only my heart, my sword and my life and I am placing them at your feet, signora! (He kneels)

Faust

(To Olympia)

Olympia

(flirtatiously) It's less—and it's more.

Mephistopheles

(Aside) Fine!

Faust

I've told you a thousand times that I would give my life for you.

Olympia

(flirtatiously) Yes—but he says it better.

Faust

(Forcefully) Olympia! (Controlling himself) Better! I don't understand.

Mephistopheles

Me neither—explain yourself?

Olympia

In his accent there's a juvenile sincerity that I don't find in you; he loves me with all the illusions of a child, and your love is more considered, more severe, in the end you are both of the same age, but he has the younger heart (To Faust) or one might say your heart is older than you are.

Faust

(Low to Mephistopheles) Ah! This past scorn pursues me forever, and they then see the wrinkles of my age through the youth of my face.

Mephistopheles

No, forget your wisdom and you will be young.

Faust

(Aloud, seeing Olympia run her hand though Valentin's hair) Olympia! Don't make me despair! Jealousy is torturing my heart, wrath is making my blood boil.

Valentin

(Rising) Take care, Signor Faust one might think you were threatening.

Mephistopheles

(Aside) Go to it, then.

Olympia

(Rising, everyone rises as well) Stop! Stop! I entreat you! I have the heart to terminate this struggle—and—to make it forgotten—completely allow me to tell you of a like adventure to ours which happened right here, 1400 years ago.

Valentin

(Coming closer) Here!

Olympia

Yes! I am not speaking of the cheerful villa which is erected on the soil we are standing; I am speaking of the ancient dwelling of Daphne, my ancestress, who sleeps here, under our feet.

Valentin

Here?

Mephistopheles

Yes (Stomping his foot) There, is a complete city; Herculaneum buried under lava, it and all its ancient masterpieces, and all its ancient marvels, and Daphne, the ancient ancestress of Olympia.

Valentin

But who knows—?

Mephistopheles

That Resina covers Herculaneum? I—who perhaps might—but later—But let's come back to this ancient ancestress.

Olympia

Just like me, she had two lovers, very taken with her beauty. The one was a savant, a philosopher I think—like you, Signor Faust—the other was—Centurion—a soldier—like you, Captain. My ancestress floated uncertainly between her two adorers, the one she was looking at was always the one she loved best—but her embarrassment was great, whenever she saw them both at the same time. Also, to finish it, as she didn't dread, as I do, hate, jealousy—and a duel—one day they were all three together (Playing with her bouquet) she threw between the rivals the flowers she held in her hand and distanced herself saying "May the conqueror bring them to me, my heart belongs to he who renders me this bouquet. (She takes a few steps to the rear and stops) She was—an evil woman that Daphne, my ancestress (She lets her bouquet drop negligently and leaves followed by the entire company. Faust and Valentin take a step toward the bouquet)

Mephistopheles

(Bending down pointing to the bouquet) The good soul! She is so indignant over the memory of her evil ancestress that she didn't even notice that this bouquet escaped from her hands. (He feigns wanting to pick up the bouquet)

Faust and Valentin

Stop!

Mephistopheles

I wanted to give it to the beautiful Olympia—one of the two of you will charge himself with that care. It's agreed, isn't it?

Valentin and Faust

It's agreed.

Mephistopheles

(Suddenly vanishing) It's agreed. (Faust and Valentin both rush to pick up the bouquet; they stop and look at each other—each at the same time placing a hand on the hilt of their sword)

Faust

I want that bouquet.

Valentin

I want it also.

Faust

(Drawing his sword) In that case.

Valentin

(Drawing his) In that case (Placing himself on guard) (Lowering his sword) A word Signor Faust.

Faust

What have we to say?

Valentin

You were born in Germany.

Faust

At Weimar—

Valentin

In Weimar—As for me, I was born there, too—

Faust

What of it?

Valentin

Listen, I've served for six years—from soldier, I've become Captain. That's because I've done my duty bravely in the face of the enemy, right?

Faust

I believe it.

Valentin

I've had three or four duels, and my hand never trembled, but this is the first time that I am fighting against a man born in the city which was also my cradle—and I have reasons about that our dwellings were perhaps neighboring. Perhaps, being children, we played together, and perhaps when still little our mothers prayed at the same time, in the same church! If we fight each other a bit later where would be the harm?

Faust

So be it, as you like it.

Valentin

(After a pause) You love Olympia?

Faust

Yes.

Valentine

You wish to bring her this bouquet?

Faust

Yes.

Valentin

Do you still have your mother?

Faust

My mother is dead.

Valentin

A sister?

Faust

I am alone in the world.

Valentin

Alone! As for me, I have a mother and a sister that I have not embraced for many long years—

I completed my term of service in Calabria, and I was going to return to them when the beauty of Calabria made me completely forget, the whitened head of the poor old woman, the blue eyes and the golden tresses of the child. I don't wish to see them with the death of a man on my heart. If I leave you this bouquet and I leave, will you think I am afraid?

Faust

No—I will think that you are better than I am.

Valentin

(Presenting the bouquet to Faust) Take it then and be happy.

Faust

(Taking it, embracing Valentin) Thanks! I love you. I love you!

Valentin

We will be friends.

Faust

We will be friends.

Valentin

(To himself) Now, I am going to find my mother and Marguerite again.

Faust

I will see you again before your departure.

Valentin

Yes, we will see each other again. (he leaves by the back, right)

Faust

He's a brave heart, and I am lucky not to have purchased the love of Olympia at the price of his life.

Olympia

(Entering—Faust presents her the bouquet) My bouquet—and Valentin?

Faust

He's leaving.

Olympia

He's leaving.

Faust

And more happy than your ancestress you will not be guilty of anyone's death.

Olympia

Ah! I wouldn't deserve that anyone expose his life for me.

Faust

It was pious memory that disarmed his arm.

Olympia

Truly? This is the day of pious works? (Chorus can be heard, Mephistopheles appears) You hear this song—these are the young girls of the North, who are coming here to accomplish a holy pilgrimage.

Mephistopheles

(Low to Olympia) And Marguerite is among them.

Olympia

The girls of your country—You, too, are not going to leave me to go see them?

Faust

What do I care about young girls—when I am here, alone with you.

Olympia

He left; they disdain me, they scorn me, they abandon me—(To Faust) Well, you, at least—speak to me of your love, make me believe it.

Faust

Oh, yes, trust me, Olympia—for Valentin's presence has been a horrible torture to my soul; for I've suffered a lot, I've wept a lot, I will weep still more at your feet—Oh! You will love me, won't you, you will love me?

Olympia

(After a gesture from Mephistopheles) Well—yes, yes, I will love you.

Mephistopheles

(Aside) Come, Marguerite, come!

Faust

Olympia, you will no longer laugh at my love; you will no longer make game of my sorrow?

Olympia

Speak, keep talking! If you knew all the suffering in the depth of my heart. They didn't love me, they lusted after me, they desired me—they didn't love me.

Faust

I love you, Olympia, I love you! These flowers that I gave you, I would have watered them with my blood, I would have paid with my life so that a word of love would escape from your lips.

Mephistopheles

(Aside) Marguerite!—There she is!

Marguerite

How is it that despite myself my steps headed in this direction?

Olympia

(Looking at Marguerite) Talk, keep talking.

Faust

For your love, I would give more than my life, I would give my soul.

Marguerite

That voice! (Turning towards Faust)

Faust

I love you! I love you!

Marguerite

(Uttering a scream) Ah!

Olympia

Look! Is it to this one, or indeed to me that you are speaking of love? (Mephistopheles and Olympia burst into laughter and disappear pointing at Faust with their finger. Then afterwards the same laughter is repeated as an echo)

Faust

Marguerite! Ah! It's the demon!

Marguerite

Faust! It's you I find again here—at the feet of another woman! (Bursts of laughter from Mephistopheles repeated by echo)

Faust

(Overwhelmed) Marguerite! (Raising his head) Well, yes, accuse me, curse me—it's vertigo, it's delirium, yes! (More laughter repeated by echo. Then Faust, forcefully) It's the demon, I tell you, who holds my soul enchained. This love is guilty, criminal, I believe it, I know it, but I cannot, do you hear, I cannot tear her out of my heart! (Takes a step to follow Olympia)

Marguerite

Henri! Are you going to abandon me again? Why you don't understand anything of what I've suffered.

Faust

Well! Let me speak to her a last time and I'll come back.

Marguerite

Oh! Don't leave me, don't leave me Henri, you are running to your ruin.

Faust

Madness.

Marguerite

No, no, it's my mother who's speaking to me—my mother that my sin killed. My mother died of shame. (Faust without listening to her heads toward the place where Olympia exited)

Valentin

(Appearing) Dead!

Faust

Madness! Madness, (Finds himself facing Valentin) Valentin!

Marguerite

Him! Him—Valentin!

Valentin

You shall not see Olympia.

Marguerite

My bro—

Valentin

(Low to Marguerite) On your life, by the memory of she who is dead, I forbid you to recognize me.

Faust

Come, you were saying something to me, Captain?

Valentin

I am saying that one mistress is enough and that I am placing myself between you and the other one.

Faust

Ah! You love Olympia? Your generosity was only a game? Get back, get back, I tell you or I will know quite well how to make passage for myself!

Valentin

(Drawing his sword) Ah! This time my hand won't tremble. (Pushing Marguerite away) I am no longer going to see my mother again. (They fight)

Marguerite

(Falling to her knees) My God! My God! For whom ought I to pray.

Mephistopheles

(Appearing as swords cross) Courage! Courage, Master Faust! Don't leave yourself open like that. The Captain is very good at fencing—it will go badly—Come, the devil must meddle. (He deflects Valentin's sword, who falls struck by Faust)

Marguerite

(Running to him) Valentin! Valentin! (She throws herself on him)

Faust

What's this mean? Marguerite—

Valentin

Marguerite—no tears—when you deviated from honor you bore me a blow more terrible—than the one which kills me—don't weep—the sleep of death is going to lead me to God—to my mother—like a soldier who did his duty. (He dies)

Marguerite

Oh! My brother! My brother!

Faust

Her brother! Her brother! Him, him—who wanted to spare me just now and that I've killed! Dead! He is dead! Wretch that I am! Marguerite! Valentin! Ah! My head's on fire—my heart's breaking! What horrible torture! Why, who then will tear me from this place? Who will give me forgetfulness?

Mephistopheles

(Putting his hand on Faust's shoulder) Me!

Faust

Well! Yes, I abandon myself to you! Save me from myself. The present horrifies me! The future dismays me.

Mephistopheles

Follow me into the past! Come! (They disappear)

CURTAIN

SCENE VIII

Herculaneum.

The stage represents a vast peristyle. The guests, lying on beds are motionless, and retain, like musicians and coryphantes, the poses in which death must have surprised them. Differing groups of marble are placed between the columns. At the back towards the middle is the statue of Helen.

Mephistopheles and Faust enter.

Mephistopheles

Here we are in Herculaneum in the house of Daphne, of that charming daughter of Lesbos who was making, in the year 79 of your era, the delight and torture of Roman youth.

Faust

(Absorbed, barely listening) Daphne—Herculaneum.

Mephistopheles

Yes, Daphne, there she is crowned with roses—and such as she was before the calamity surprised her like lightning. She was giving a feast to celebrate the arrival of a magnificent marble that you see here.

Faust

That—that marble.

Mephistopheles

It's the statue of Helen of Troy.

Faust

Helen! She's the first poetry; she's the first passion of my youth.

Mephistopheles

Truly?

Faust

How many times in the feverish nights that succeeded study did I dream that this blonde daughter of Greece—would revive beneath the ardor of my love!

Mephistopheles

(Aside) Ah! This is fine. (Aloud) So you remember your youthful years?

Faust

Yes, but it's strange—between that time and the time we now are—there's an emptiness in my spirit that I cannot succeed in filling.

Mephistopheles

You asked me for forgetfulness and I gave it to you?

Faust

Forgetfulness?

Mephistopheles

Forgetfulness of a recent sorrow, forgetfulness for some hours and you see, I plunged you into the bosom of the past. Say a word and a whole world is going to be reborn for you alone and the interrupted songs are anew going to shake these arches. Order, and the smile that Daphne didn't have the time to complete will be reborn under your glance, and will come, if you wish, to expire on your lips.

Faust

Well, yes, let ancient intoxication whirl before my dazzled eyes!

Mephistopheles

In that case be satisfied. (At these words everything comes to life and motion, and the guests finish the bacchic song at the note interrupted and at the same time dances linked to several refrains)

Chorus

Intoxicate with burning breath
Spread over me your dreams of good
Friends, let's empty our full cups
Let's drink to fill them again.

Daphne

Greetings to Master Faust.

Faust

You know me?

Mephistopheles

(Low to Daphne) You see, his memory is really dozing. It began with seduction and murder.

Daphne

(Laughing) Now, he's mine to make a pagan of him.

Faust

Why this gaiety?

Daphne

I'm laughing about you, Signor.

Faust

About me?

Daphne

Imagine, Cneia, that this fine gentleman is coming to us from a strange world, where the sun is pale, those who live there lack gold, perfumes, light, and flowers—what they call their summer would be more like our winter. And they live so little, that we dead are more living than their tombs.

Faust

That, perhaps is true; what you said there, my beautiful scoffer.

Daphne

Do they even know how to love? To love! (She laughs) Imagine a crepuscular soul, something somber and sickly all charged with terrors and remorse. But that fire, that real fire that sparkles in Helen's eyes, that love which was the despair of Asia and the enchantment of Greece—that flame which in an instant confounded in the same fire heaven and earth—men and gods—(Pointing to Faust) that I, Cneia, will never know .

Faust

You think so?

Daphne

Ah! If a spark from this fire of the world could one day penetrate his veins; if from the top of its golden arrow love inoculated you a bit with breath from her lips a bit of delirium from her glance.

Faust

Daphne.

Daphne

You would then be equal to the gods; you would know what it is to love.

Faust

Why, I feel it! Why, I am experiencing it that delirium! Where am I? And what's taking place in me? Daphne, I feel your words caressing my memories like perfume come from the valleys of Lesbos. (Heatedly) A cup! A cup! Let me empty it to you charming marble, where the poetry of love sing together completely. (He receives a cup from the hands of a slave) To you also, smiling and handsome gods—to you who animate nature and transmit to all things your divine beauty.

All

Evohe! Evohe! (Marguerite appears and comes forward to the right)

Daphne

(To Mephistopheles) Marguerite! (She disappears)

Faust

Who are you?

Marguerite

Don't you recognize me?

Faust

You?

Mephistopheles

(Aside, extending his hand to him) You asked me for forgetfulness.

Faust

No!

Marguerite

What! This face which used to make you smile, these eyes you made shed so many tears, you don't even recognize them?

Faust

(Searching) No—but talk—keep talking—

Marguerite

Faust! I am the one you loved—I am the one you loaded with bitterness and sorrows, the one whose soul you tore to shreds, and who has not ceased to pray for you! Faust!—I am Marguerite!

Faust

Marguerite! Marguerite!—This is strange—your name, which awakens no memory in my head, resonates dolorously in my bosom. It seems that my heart recalls and that my memory has forgotten—my eyes rest on yours, as on the eyes of friends, and yet I don't remember you!

Marguerite

Faust!

Faust

Your voice makes me shiver, your tears make mine flow, my soul rushes completely towards your soul (Gesture by Mephistopheles) and yet I don't recognize you.

Marguerite

(After having cast a glance at Mephistopheles and recognized him) Ah!—Well! We will struggle together and you will triumph.

Faust

(Eyes fixed on hers, searching) Yes, yes—I wish to—!

Mephistopheles

(Aside) And as for me, I don't wish to. (Aloud, addressing the statue) Help me, marvel of the genius of Phidias! Daughter of Jupiter, arise and walk—! Look, Faust, it's Helen who's reviving and who will live again for you.

Faust

Helen! Helen!

Marguerite

My God! My God!

Faust

Oh! Miracle of art, who become suddenly a miracle of nature! Marble in which breathes the reawakened soul of Helen! Supreme beauty, grace divine and unspeakable—I love you and I prostrate myself at your feet.

Mephistopheles

Come on, there he is—I think—as fine a pagan as one could wish.

Marguerite

Faust—remember that God made you to adore your mother.

Faust

There is no other adoration—there is no other cult than the cult of beauty. (In the distance can be heard the roll of thunder and the deafening noise of the eruption of Vesuvius. Night begins to come on)

Marguerite

Well—you will see how people cursed by the Lord perish; you will see this new Gomorrah collapse and fall under the divine wrath—these worshippers of infamous gods.

CURTAIN

SCENE IX

The columns and walls collapse and allow the city in ruins to be seen. Vesuvius vomits lava which spreads everywhere—everything vanishes except Faust and Mephistopheles—shouts of desolation.

Mephistopheles

Well, my Master, I gave you youth, you seduced innocence; I poured you the cup of love—you found in it only intoxication and blood—and even in your dreams you've renounced your God! Are you really mine? Answer!

Faust

Not yet. You promised me riches, power. I want them! It's through them I can save myself!

CURTAIN

SCENE X

In the Indies.

A public square—to the left, near the audience, the entrance to a palace.

Wagner and Fridolin arrive from different sides. They are borne in rich palanquins and accompanied by chief porters.

Wagner

(Descending from his palanquin) Gently, my friends, gently, I am very delicate.

Fridolin

As gently as possible. Take the greatest care of me.

Wagner

Now, withdraw.

Fridolin

(Giving them a large purse) Here, share this money between you that I am giving you in the name of the great Maharajah. (They bow and leave. Strollers at the back)

Wagner

Maharajah! Now here's Señor Faust become sovereign of this country, and me, superintendent of his charities.

Fridolin

And I, what am I?

Wagner

You are the subintendent of the superintendent.

Fridolin

Signor Faust brought us here with him. He casts away gold on broad daylight and we are charged with spreading his bounties.

Wagner

And of gathering for him the most blessings possible. I've received enough of them today, and I won't be put out to talk with my beautiful slave.

Fridolin

Then I'm clearing out.

Wagner

Why?

Fridolin

I cannot put up with her, your beautiful slave.

Wagner

Oh! But you don't have to—she's really changed—she now maintains all the sweetness of the demi-sex of which she's now a part.

Fridolin

A demi-sex?

Wagner

Yes, the wife—the demi-sex.

Fridolin

Ah! Right.

Wagner

Since then, she's become so docile, so obedient.

Fridolin

Truly? She's obedient?

Wagner

Perfectly obedient—she does whatever I wish.

Fridolin

Is it possible?

Wagner

It's I, I who command; now she obeys my least desires.

Fridolin

Ah! Yes—in that case she's really changed.

Wagner

But where is she?

Sulphurine

I'm right here.

Wagner

That's very fortunate (Severely) I told you to remain and wait for me here.

Sulphurine

That's true, but it pleased me to leave.

Wagner

Ah!

Fridolin

She's prepared.

Wagner

It pleased you.

Sulphurine

To leave.

Wagner

That works quite well; I had a place to send you outside. Huh!—how prepared she is! She obeys even what I had the intention of ordering.

Fridolin

She's—superb.

Wagner

And where did you go little one?

Sulphurine

Where I wanted.

Wagner

Exactly where I was going to send you.

Fridolin

How that works again.

Wagner

And now, you are going to stay with me?

Sulphurine

No.

Wagner

Ah—you—you are leaving again—

Sulphurine

Yes—

Wagner

And when will you return?

Sulphurine

When it suits me.

Wagner

So be it—But not very late, not very late—or I'll be annoyed, (She turns her back on him) You see that I speak as master, I've assumed my role.

Fridolin

You've done well—And how she listens to you!

Sulphurine

Have you executed the orders of Signor Faust?

Fridolin

Yes, we have.

Sulphurine

Shut up—

Fridolin

Excuse me—

Sulphurine

I wish it.

Fridolin

Oh, but see here, as for me, I am not your master, you have no right to give orders to me.

Wagner

Look—enough, Fridolin! She wishes it! Yes, Sulphurine, the orders of Master Faust are executed—he told us: Help the miserable and I think I've been able enough—

Fridolin

And I, too! I assembled all the butcher—boys—the weavers, the baker boys, I gave 1,000 pieces of gold to each, and they are happy. They are going to establish everything on their own account—they are going to be masters in their turn.

Wagner

All! Ah, indeed!—Where will they find lads to work.

Fridolin

Lads—? As for me, I don't know—they'll do it—

Sulphurine

Good, good, that's their concern.

Wagner

That's fair! I did as much for the tailors, the woodcutters and other bodies of state. Only I was more generous than Fridolin. They won't set up their own business, not mine, they will live in their small incomes. They will all be men of property.

Fridolin

All—Ah! We are great philanthropists!

Wagner

We will soon gather general blessings.

Sulphurine

(Ironic) And Signor Faust will be pleased with you. (Shouting at the entry)

Voices

Long live the Maharajah! Long live the Maharajah!

Faust

(Entering) Enough! Enough!

Fridolin

Long live the Mah—

Faust

Will you be silent!

Wagner

One would say that your lordship is irritated against us—

Sulphurine

He's got plenty of reason to.

Faust

You've wrecked, ruined everything.

Wagner

Us?

Faust

Fools that you are—you wanted to enrich the world and you've killed work.

Wagner

(Aside) That's possible but he didn't have a hard life.

Faust

Under weight of gold you've suffocated, strength, energy, courage—! You've killed work and dishonored riches. (He moves away)

Wagner

Poor riches—here you are dishonored.

Fridolin

All the same I am not uneasy over his fate; there will still be found a few good souls who won't repulse it.

Wagner

Come on, come on, I see what it is, we should only have given money to those who don't need it. (Great noises of fanfares)

Wagner and Fridolin

What's that? (General movement)

Sulphurine

(To Faust) Signor! The Maharajah of neighboring states is coming to visit you.

Faust

Indeed, I ordered a feast to receive him.

Sulphurine

Yes, but they have so cleverly executed your orders that your servants are now too rich to wish to serve others. (Enter Mephistopheles in the brilliant costume of a Maharajah, leaning on two slaves preceded and followed by people of his entourage)

Mephistopheles

Glory and blessing to the powerful Maharajah, my brother (He bows)

Faust

May Your Lordship pardon me, but for—(Looking at him in the face) You!

Mephistopheles

Myself—Don't put yourself out—if to receive me you have neither bouquet nor feast, in default of your slaves and your servants we have mine.

Faust

Yours?

Mephistopheles

The rest of my suite that I left a few miles from here—so much was I in haste to see you again.

Faust

Ah! You have subjects?

Mephistopheles

(To all) Yes, I'm coming to see you as a good neighbor (To Faust) to ask you what you have done with your riches that I gave you, and if you have piously repurchased your past.

Faust

(To all) Let us be left alone. (They leave—the suite of Mephistopheles remains on stage)

Mephistopheles

You have to speak to me?

Faust

Yes, you deceived me.

Mephistopheles

Me?

Faust

If I desired riches it was because I was jostled in youth and in love by all the obstacles of passion, because to repurchase myself, I wanted to assuage all the wretched and dry their tears; for this I needed inexhaustible treasures.

Mephistopheles

(Forcefully) I gave you them.

Faust

What I asked of you—was riches without equal.

Mephistopheles

I gave it to you.

Faust

You lie!

Mephistopheles

Me? Ah!

Faust

There is in this country someone whose wealth crushes mine, whose power makes mine pale.

Mephistopheles

Of whom are you speaking?

Faust

Of a woman.

Mephistopheles

Her name?

Faust

I'm ignorant of that, they call her saint or good angel.

Mephistopheles

She's too good to be of my acquaintance.

Faust

Everywhere I go to spread alms, her steps have preceded mine, her praise is in every mouth—it's she, always she, who is blessed! This charity is ceaselessly opposed to mine—it's a torture to me. I suffer at the thought that the good deeds of another are placing her name above mine. This charity, of which they sing such high praise, humiliates my heart and revolts my—

Mephistopheles

Your pride.

Faust

(Forcefully) Well, yes, my pride!—Pride of goodness, do you hear, demon? It's not that which got you driven from heaven.

Mephistopheles

(Low, calm) And it's not that which will open its gates for you—(Aloud) It's always pride.

Faust

I want to satiate it.

Mephistopheles

Well—but—you are Master of your state. It's necessary to reserve to yourself alone the right of charity; to forbid the sale of virtue—and to reserve to yourself a monopoly of it, like salt and tobacco.

Faust

Enough! (Violent roaring is heard. Wagner appears) What's the matter?

Wagner

Milord, these are folks satiated with your generous benefactions who are soliciting the grace of seeing you—a bit abruptly.

Faust

Let them come (Wagner leaves)

Mephistopheles

And this time, I suppose it's your name that you will hear blessed, and not that of your rival. (Enter a large group of men who are speaking excitedly and push Wagner)

Faust

Why these shouts? What's happening?

First Man

Lord, the gold your servants threw so blindly have spread disorder everywhere—

Faust

(With energy) I know it—I will repair the fault they have committed—what more are you requesting?

Second Man

The gold you yourself have spread among us has spread misfortune and despair among us.

Faust

Me! Me! (Forcefully) Explain yourself, speak—I wish it.

Third Man

Take that money back, Milord; it has driven peace and happiness from my house, and even fraternal tenderness. It has cost amongst my children division, wrath and hate.

Faust

Hate! (The second man approaches him) What do you want with me?

Second Man

Your gold has troubled my reason and withered my heart -- suddenly becoming rich without the bother of work, I threw myself into idleness and vice. I abandoned my wife, and my wife died—it's the work of this gold you gave me. (He casts it away in despair)

Faust

(Beside himself) Enough! Enough! Why then there's a curse on each of my good deeds. (He meets the look of Mephistopheles who laughs) Oh! Yes, yes, it's the gold of the cursed! (A young woman emerges from the crowd holding a child by the hand) What do you want with me, woman? Are you also coming to reproach me once more with sorrow, despair, death.

Young Woman

No, Lord, I am coming to thank you.

Faust

(With joy) Ah!

Young Woman

You wanted to succor me and it's not your fault if I didn't come until now.

Faust

Indeed, I recognize you, poor woman! Fire had destroyed your dwelling, it had consumed your harvest, and to complete the misfortune, your child was dying. I said to you—come to me. Why have you delayed until today?

Young Woman

There was another who came to us, Milord.

Faust

Another?

Mephistopheles

(With irony) The saint, perhaps.

Faust

And what did she do for you?

Young Woman

What did she do?—She spent by my son tiring days and sleepless nights—lavishing the most touching care on him. The child could not sleep but he seemed to understand her tears; she shed tears of compassion in response to his tears. I thought they were two angels speaking in an unknown tongue and I fell to my knees before them. One day the tears diminished and smiles returned to both of them. My care and my wakefulness did not suffice; a mother alone does not always obtain from heaven her child's life—but mine had two mothers and God gave him back to me. (She embraces her child)

Faust

And this woman? This woman?

Young Woman

You don't know her—? She's—

Mephistopheles

She's the saint, right?

Young Woman

Yes—

Faust

Always, always her—

Mephistopheles

(Low) Always—(Laughs)

Faust

Enough!—And the ravages of the fire?

Young Woman

Oh! Everything is repaired.

Faust

Why in that case she is quite rich?

Young Woman

No, Lord, she is poor like us.

Faust

Poor?

Young Woman

But at her prayer, all our neighbors rushed to our assistance—each of them gave a little of his time and the house was rebuilt, each gave some portion of his harvest and our losses were repaired. She is poor Milord, and yet she spreads riches in her path, because faith accompanies her and charity is engendered by her voice.

Faust

Poor—and her charity cures all wounds, consoles all hearts, while mine only bears bitter fruit. I wish to see this woman: let her come to my palace.

Young Woman

She won't come, Milord.

Faust

Even if I order her?

Young Woman

She never enters except into the dwellings of the poor. She won't come.

Faust

Well! I will enrich those who bring her to me by force. Go! Let me be obeyed. (Several men bow and leave)

Mephistopheles

Marvelous! (Uproar of fanfares) But hear fanfares announcing the arrival of my subjects. (To all) And now—Pleasure (To Faust) after charity. (A procession enters) (A ballet) (After the ballet a dull murmur. Successive shouts and voices repeat on all sides)

Voices

The Saint—Glory to the Saint.

Faust

What's wrong?

Mephistopheles

It's she they are bringing—that woman you gave the order to be brought here.

Faust

The Saint! Finally I am going to see her! (Enter Marguerite veiled, with guards. At the sight of Marguerite all the wretched kneel—the others bow)

Faust

Who are you? (She raises her veil) Marguerite! She!

Mephistopheles

(With a scornful motion) I am leaving you, friend Faust, I am leaving you with this angel; ask her, her secret.

Faust

Goodbye, accursed one, goodbye.

Mephistopheles

(Mounting the palanquin which just entered) Don't even say that word to me: between men and the devil it's always: *au revoir*!

The Poor

Glory to the Saint!

Mephistopheles's Followers

Glory to the Maharajah (The cortège resumes its march. The

actors freeze)

CURTAIN

SCENE XI

Inside Faust's Palace.

Fridolin

(Alone) Decidedly fortune has turned everybody's head. Master Wagner, who recognized the danger of giving too liberally, has taken care to keep everything for himself. Lord Faust has become somber and sad, distrusting everyone and no one approaches him except through interest. Ah! Vile metal! Wretched money! From what I have amassed, I will retire from the world so as to no longer hear it spoken of. And then, I'm weary of the life that I'm leading here with Master Wagner and this little monstrosity of a Sulphurine that he created.

Voice of Sulphurine

Thanks!

Fridolin

Huh? Who's speaking to me?

Sulphurine

(Appearing) Thanks, Lord Fridolin!

Fridolin

What! It's you?

Sulphurine

Yes, I am very much at ease to have surprised your thoughts and the secret of your heart.

Fridolin

The secret of my heart; I don't know what it is.

Sulphurine

Oh! I know what it is, I do! I know you hate me. (Aside) And you will pay me dearly for it!

Fridolin

I hate you, I—Hush! Listen here, you are not nice.

Sulphurine

Ah!—You think so—

Fridolin

I really want you to be willful, jealous, spiteful, coquettish—you're a woman—but it's not only that—

Sulphurine

Is it my fault you didn't create me better?

Fridolin

I don't say that, but—

Sulphurine

Is it not Master Wagner who is guilty?

Fridolin

That's true enough, but—

Sulphurine

As for me, I don't ask better than to be me, but I wasn't made that way.

Fridolin

Yes, some ingredients were neglected.

Sulphurine

As for me, I'd ask nothing better than to be sweet, loving—but for whom? Master Wagner is not handsome.

Fridolin

He does look villainous.

Sulphurine

He's not witty.

Fridolin

He's a wine bottle.

Sulphurine

Ah! If he were young and sweet—like you—!

Fridolin

Huh?

Sulphurine

Lovable like you.

Fridolin

Like—like me—don't say stupid things.

Sulphurine

If he were witty like you—

Fridolin

Sulphurine! Sulphurine!

Sulphurine

It would be a pleasure to be obedient.

Fridolin

Yes, I understand that I would only order you to do pleasant things.

Sulphurine

It would have been happiness to show myself sweet, loving.

Fridolin

Yes—I—I understand that as well.

Sulphurine

Oh! What a difference between you and him.

Fridolin

(Aside) She's got taste, the little one (Aloud) Look Sulphurine—you find me agreeable.

Sulphurine

Alas! Yes—but you hate me—

Fridolin

Why, no!

Sulphurine

Why, yes!

Fridolin

Why, no!

Sulphurine

Why, yes!

Fridolin

Why, no, I don't hate you—you are nice—I've never looked at you so well—you are very pretty, Sulphurine—and you say that I hate you. Come on—why, I—on the contrary, why, I love you.

Sulphurine

You!—Ah! If I could believe you.

Fridolin

Believe me, believe it, Sulphurine!—Yes, it's only now that I understand what's taking place inside me—this hate, Sulphurine, it was, from love, from jealousy, from frenzy—Oh! Yes, I love you, I adore you Sulphurine! I swear it to you—here I swear it to you at your knees.

Sulphurine

(Aside) Here we go! (Aloud) But, I am not free, my life, my being, my heart all belong to my master.

Fridolin

Your heart! It's not true! A turtle dove's heart a very small heart that I purchased myself. He didn't reimburse me for it, he doesn't dispose of it.

Sulphurine

Oh! So long as he lives, I will be his slave!

Fridolin

You! His slave!

Sulphurine

So long as he lives—and afterwards—(Extending her hand to him) Perhaps—

Fridolin

(With intoxication) Perhaps!—but he can last a long while.

Sulphurine

(Sadly) Alas!—I fear not—

Fridolin

(Sadly) What? That poor Wagner does his life only hang by a thread?

Sulphurine

Less than that: a hair—

Fridolin

A hair! A mere hair?

Sulphurine

Yes, it's a long white hair—that he wears on his face—to which his destiny is attached.

Fridolin

And if he loses that hair?

Sulphurine

I will have the misfortune of being free.

Fridolin

Oh! The poor man—! You will point it out to me, Sulphurine?

Sulphurine

What?

Fridolin

That big white hair.

Sulphurine

(Aside) I was sure of it. (Wagner's voice is heard off)

Sulphurine

Hush!—That's him—act so he won't suspect what I am experiencing.

Fridolin

Yes, deceive him—for his repose.

Wagner

(Entering) Ah! I'm harassed, broken with weariness—I would really like a seat.

Sulphurine

(Very bustling) A seat?—Here's one, Master—

Wagner

Thanks. What—what—it's you who are serving me, Sulphurine?

Sulphurine

Am I not your slave?

Wagner

I know that indeed; but ordinarily, isn't it Fridolin?

Fridolin

Yes, yes, ordinarily—but it seems things are changing—

Wagner

I came in great haste! Ah! How hot I am! I would really like—you know—one of those useful objects—decorated with feathers.

Fridolin

We don't have any.

Sulphurine

A fly chaser—! Here's one, Master.

Wagner

Give me.

Sulphurine

Not at all! I want myself—

Wagner

Again? But I'm not coming back to it again!

Sulphurine

(Fanning him) See how worn out he is!

Wagner

Oh—quite worn out—

Sulphurine

How hot he is. (She dries his face)

Wagner

She's overwhelming me with little attentions. Are you sick, Sulphurine?

Sulphurine

(Amorously looking at Fridolin) No, it's not that—

Fridolin

(Aside) As for me, I know what it is.

Wagner

Ah, what a delightful temperature this produces—Ah, how good it is. Ah!—How good it is—! Come closer, little one!

Sulphurine

Yes, Master.

Wagner

(Aside) It seems to me good to command—for the good. (Aloud) Come closer, also, Fridolin.

Fridolin

(Hypocritically) Yes, my sweet Master. (They place themselves on each side of his chair)

Wagner

Ah! I feel happy amidst my faithful servants.

Fridolin

(Angrily, aside) Servant!—She (Looking at Wagner's skull) Heavens, you have a white hair.

Sulphurine

(Low) That's it.

Fridolin

(Low) Ah!

Wagner

Sulphurine, I want to reward you for your submission, for your eagerness to serve me—I want you to know my tender feelings for you.

Sulphurine

Your feelings, Master?

Wagner

Yes, Fridolin—tell her to what degree I love her.

Fridolin

(Jealous) Me?

Wagner

Tell her how much I idolize her—tell her—

Fridolin

(With rage) What me—That I—(Calming down) What a villainous gray hair—

Wagner

A hair? What hair?

Fridolin

(Indicating it) A hair that you have there—it displeases me!

Wagner

Well—pull it out!

Fridolin

Pull it out! You want for me to—me, pull it out for you?

Wagner

Certainly, since it spoils my looks—you know quite well I want to be pleasing to Sulphurine.

Sulphurine

(Modestly) Please me!

Fridolin

(With concentrated rage) Please her—to her—(He grabs the hair) Come on then.

Wagner

Pull, why pull it will you? I don't want anything to re-chill her tenderness.

Fridolin

Her tenderness—I'm pulling. (He pulls the hair which stretches and grows at the same time)

Wagner

What are you doing?

Fridolin

(Terrified) I'm pulling, I'm pulling.

Wagner

Ah! Ah! Ah! That tickles me.

Fridolin

I'm pulling again—but it doesn't break—why it's growing—it keeps growing—

Wagner

Ah—bah—

Fridolin

And it's getting fatter.

Wagner

(Looking at the hair that keeps growing) What's that I see there? Goodness!—That's my hair there?

Fridolin

(Still pulling beside himself) It's got one strong root, Sir—and it keeps coming—this overwhelms me! Horror! I feel my wits wandering—Ah, I'm going crazy—Let's flee—(He leaves still holding the hair)

Wagner

Fridolin! Fridolin! Stop pulling wretch. (Leaves running after

Fridolin)

Sulphurine

I am avenged, Fridolin—If your soul is not lost it's well hazarded.

Faust

(Entering) Alone! Always alone! This distrust I've conceived for all those around me is a torture to my heart. Marguerite (To Sulphurine) Where is she?

Sulphurine

There—in prayer.

Faust

I wish she could see me such as I was before. Ah, if I could obtain her forgiveness! Here she is. (Marguerite appears—he gestures to Sulphurine to retire. Exit Sulphurine)

Marguerite

Why have you brought me here by violence? I went wherever misfortune is found, everywhere there was suffering, everywhere danger appeared, and I went freely.

Faust

Marguerite, you can still save me.

Marguerite

You are mistaken, Faust, your salvation depends on you alone.

Faust

Don't abandon me, take pity on me.

Marguerite

It's God's pity you ought to implore.

Faust

Listen—return to me the heart I disdained and I will consecrate my whole life to you—all my soul.

Marguerite

Will you return to me my mother who is dead?

Faust

Marguerite!

Marguerite

Will you return to me my brother who you killed?

Faust

Marguerite, your soul is pious, your heart is charitable, and you said it, I am wretched, I weep! Oh! Don't repulse me. If you wish it, I will share my riches with you—you will borrow from my treasures to succor those who suffer.

Marguerite

The source of your treasures is impure.

Faust

Oh! I entreat you to have pity on my sufferings, do not irritate me with new scorn—and if you disdain my love, don't add to the bitterness of my soul, don't push me to despair, don't disdain my wrath.

Marguerite

I didn't bend before your tears—what can you do to me with your threats?

Faust

(Forcefully) Still, still implacable. But you are not thinking that all here bend under my will and obey my gesture? I can—

Marguerite

Poor fool! There is no power on earth that can shake the faith which animates me.

Faust

No power on earth—and beyond it?

Marguerite

Heaven!

Faust

No, no, heaven won't listen to me.

Marguerite

Faust.

Faust

But Hell!

Marguerite

Shut up!

Faust

If you repulse me and brave me, I can—I can call to help me, a power—

Marguerite

Henri!

Faust

Marguerite, I love you. Will you give me your love?

Marguerite

Never!

Faust

Never! Well! I am going to finish with these obstacles that are ceaselessly heaped in front of me! I want a power which will bend, which will break, which will destroy—! I want power enough to be equal at last of Satan himself! Help me, spirit of evil! (One hears an infernal noise. The stage darkens—)

BLACKOUT

SCENE XII

A desolate place.

Mephistopheles

(Appearing suddenly) I am here!

Faust

Where am I? Where have you taken me?

Mephistopheles

On the highest summit of Broken, on Walpurgis Night—Come on, come.

Marguerite

Faust, you are abandoning me again; under the features of a pure angel, object of your first love, your guardian is hidden. (Her female clothes vanish and are replaced by those of an angel)

Faust

You!

Marguerite

(As Angel) To attempt to save you I took on the features of Marguerite, and I followed you into each of these countries where your vagabond passion dragged you.

Faust

But what has become of her?

Mephistopheles

You want to know? Well, Marguerite, abandoned by you, lost her mind, and in her madness killed her infant!

Faust

Great God!

Mephistopheles

And now she's plunged in a dungeon, her sentence given, and the executioner awaits her.

Faust

Death and destruction to you, monster! I want you to save her.

Mephistopheles

At what price, my Master?

Faust

Take my life, take my soul—but save her.

Mephistopheles

Your soul!—At last—deal made—Ah! Ah! Ah! Let's leave.

(At the back. Death appears, whose deployed wings support Faust and Mephistopheles—they vanish in the air—Marguerite leaves—A moment later the stage is invaded by demons and goblins. A dance infernal)

CURTAIN

SCENE XIII

A cell.

Marguerite is lying on a pallet.

Faust

(Led in by Mephistopheles) It's here that she is suffering and that she's weeping—for a sin that is mine!—and you dragged me far from her; you threw me into your shameful orgies, while all abandoned she saw death ready to strike her.

Mephistopheles

Fine—she's not the first.

Faust

She's not the first!—Execrable monster! The thought that Marguerite is sharing the fate of a thousand others makes you smile.

Mephistopheles

Is this finished?

Faust

Oh! Why am I coupled with this odious companion?

Mephistopheles

Can't you get thunder to obliterate me? Think a bit sooner?

Faust

You agreed to save her!

Mephistopheles

I am not all powerful on earth and in heaven! I cannot open bolts, nor turn away the vengeance of your laws. I've put to sleep the vigilance of the jailor and you possessed yourself of the keys to this prison—I will watch, the enchanted horses are ready; I will lead you to each other; there my power stops.

Marguerite

(Waking up) To die! To die!

Faust

She's waking up.

Mephistopheles

Prepare her to follow you—hurry—hurry— (He leaves)

Marguerite

(Raising herself up and looking about with distraction) Someone!—Are they coming to get me? Oh! You have compassion for my misery!

Faust

Oh! Poor Marguerite!

Marguerite

Marguerite! Who uttered that name? There used to be a Marguerite, I knew her—she was a pure and well behaved girl; her heart was completely filled with three holy affections! God—her mother and her brother! Another one came—Faust! Faust!—He installed himself in this heart and he drove out first mother and mother died, then he drove out Valentin and Valentin died, too. But God—he cannot drive him out, and my poor heart is broken in the struggle and it's Marguerite who's dead in her turn.

Faust

(Trembling) Ah! Wretch that I am—and—your child—poor woman.

Marguerite

My child? A beautiful child—go—one day—I was seated by the lake—I was waiting—I was always waiting. The little one looked laughing through the rushes; I looked, too; there was on the surface of the water a little angel who was smiling at my son—I approached him, he approached likewise. The child held his hands out to him, and he held them out, too. I thought it was God who was demanding my son of me, and I let him slip softly into the arms of his angel. The lake opened, then it shut again and they vanished together! The angel had carried away my child and God hasn't given him back to me yet.

Faust

No, Marguerite! It's not you, it's my abandonment that killed this poor victim.

Marguerite

(With distraction) Listen, I thought I heard Henri's voice.

Faust

Ah, if at least, you could recognize me, if at least I could get you out of here! Marguerite why turn your glance toward mine, recall your memory; recognize me at last. Marguerite, Marguerite!

Marguerite

Ah, yes, yes—it's his voice, it's his voice.

Faust

It's me, I tell you, I who love you still and am coming to save you.

Marguerite

Him! It's him! My God! Ah! How happy I am! Where are my sufferings? Where are my anguishes? Where are my tears? There is no more prison, there are no more chains! He's with me, and here I am saved.

Faust

Come! Come!

Marguerite

Where are you going? Wait—don't move away—Stay, stay, stay—I am really here where you are! I am so happy like this. (She leans her head on Faust's breast)

Faust

Each moment of delay brings a new danger. Follow me, that's my only prayer.

Marguerite

Why aren't you pressing me in your arms like before? Can you no longer embrace me? Did you forget already?

Faust

I love as I used to love you—but we must leave—we must take a step—take a step and you are free—

Marguerite

Free! Free!—Let's leave.

Mephistopheles

(Reappearing at the door) Come on, you are lost.

Marguerite

(Recoiling in horror) Ah!

Mephistopheles

No more delay—no more useless words—my horses are

stamping with impatience, and day begins to break.

Marguerite

It's him! Him! Drive him away, Henri, drive him away.

Faust

I want you to live.

Marguerite

(Falling on her knees) All powerful God! Good God! God filled with mercy—it's to you that I confide myself.

Mephistopheles

They are coming—the guards, the judges, and the executioner—hurry or I will be forced to abandon the two of you.

Faust

Marguerite! You haven't stopped loving me! Marguerite, don't you want to live?

Marguerite

I love you, Henri; I love you, and I want to die.

Faust

What are you saying?

Marguerite

I want to die to appease the divine wrath, to die to repurchase your salvation and mine.

Faust

Well! I will tear you out of here, despite yourself. (he seizes her in his arms)

Marguerite

(Struggling) No—no—down there in the door way, with him, Henri, with him—(Pointing to Mephistopheles) that's eternal torture—those are the eternal tortures of hell—I don't wish it, I don't wish it. (She falls) Ah!

Faust

Marguerite!

Marguerite

Ah! God heard my prayers! He had pity on my tears—my sacrifice is accepted—you wanted to see me free, Henri, be satisfied (Falling) I am free—I am free! (She dies)

Faust

Ah! Marguerite is dead! Marguerite is dead! (He falls kneeling next to her)

CURTAIN

SCENE XIV

Apotheosis.

The stage represents: on high—paradise; below: the entrance to hell! In the foreground Mephistopheles—Faust kneeling by the bed. Four angels raise and bear the body of Marguerite.

Faust

Marguerite!

Mephistopheles

She's been judged now. (The angel of the Lord appears and points to Marguerite)

Angel

She is saved. (To Mephistopheles) Get the behind me, accursed! (Mephistopheles vanishes) (To Faust who remains kneeling) Let the sinner repent. An angel is praying for him—

CURTAIN

ABOUT THE AUTHOR

FRANK J. MORLOCK has written and translated many plays since retiring from the legal profession in 1992. His translations have also appeared on Project Gutenberg, the Alexandre Dumas Père web page, Literature in the Age of Napoléon, Infinite Artistries.com, and Munsey's (formerly Blackmask). In 2006 he received an award from the North American Jules Verne Society for his translations of Verne's plays. He lives and works in México.

www.ingramcontent.com/pod-product-compliance
Lightning Source LLC
LaVergne TN
LVHW041617070426
835507LV00008B/304